# MILE MARKERS OF LIFE

# MILE MARKERS OF LIFE

A 100-Day Christian Devotional
for Direction and Strength

KEYIMANI ALFORD

**Mile Markers of Life: A 100-Day Christian Devotional for Direction and Strength**

Copyright © 2025 by Keyimani L. Alford

All rights reserved. No portion of this book may be reproduced, stored in a retrieval system, or transmitted in any form or by any means—electronic, mechanical, photocopying, recording, or otherwise—except for brief quotations in critical articles or reviews, without prior written permission of the publisher.

Published by Keywords Unlocked, LLC
6969 N. Port Washington Road, Suite B150, PMB 1025
Glendale, Wisconsin 53217
www.keywordsunlocked.com
keywordsunlockedllc@gmail.com

For information about discounts or bulk purchases for educational, church, corporate, or nonprofit use, please email keywordsunlockedllc@gmail.com.

Scripture quotations are from The Holy Bible, New International Version® (NIV), New Living Translation® (NLT), English Standard Version® (ESV), and King James Version (KJV), public domain), used by permission where applicable.

Cover and interior design by Keywords Unlocked, LLC.
Printed in the United States of America.

10 9 8 7 6 5 4 3 2 1

Library of Congress Control Number has been applied for.

ISBN: 979-8-9990953-7-4 (Paperback)
ISBN: 979-8-9990953-8-1 (Hardcover)

*For my friend Traci,
whose heart knows both love and loss.
When the future may feel uncertain,
may you remember God still holds every mile of your journey.*

# CONTENTS

**Introduction** | MM 00: The Beginning — xiii
**Day 01** | MM 304: Traveling Tires — 1
**Day 02** | MM 287.4: Spared — 3
**Day 03** | MM 301.8: Trust — 5
**Day 04** | MM 261.2: Silence — 7
**Day 05** | MM 300.4: Shifting Circles — 9
**Day 06** | MM 249.2: Peace in Chaos — 11
**Day 07** | MM 268.4: The Gift of Consistency — 13
**Day 08** | MM 254.4: Small Joys — 15
**Day 09** | MM 302.2: Endurance — 17
**Day 10** | MM 292.8: Letting Go — 19
**Day 11** | MM 286.6: Perspective Shift — 21
**Day 12** | MM 300.2: Familiar Roads, New Lessons — 23
**Day 13** | MM 245.4: The Power of Stillness — 25
**Day 14** | MM 260.4: The Cost of Sacrifice — 27
**Day 15** | MM 269.8: Learning to Pivot — 29
**Day 16** | MM 247.2: Finding Focus — 31
**Day 17** | MM 263.6: Shattered Glass — 33
**Day 18** | MM 248.8: The Yacht on My Screen — 35
**Day 19** | MM 259.8: Know Your Worth — 37
**Day 20** | MM 284.8: Seasons and Sacrifice — 39
**Day 21** | MM 303: The Choice is Yours — 41
**Day 22** | MM 302: Making Room — 43

| | | |
|---|---|---|
| Day 23 | MM 294.2: The Season of Ideas | 45 |
| Day 24 | MM 265.2: Your Assignment | 47 |
| Day 25 | MM 275.6: What I Trust | 49 |
| Day 26 | MM 250.2: Facing Yourself | 51 |
| Day 27 | MM 258.4: What Sustains You | 53 |
| Day 28 | MM 276.2: The Three D's | 55 |
| Day 29 | MM 262.6: The Cost of Haste | 57 |
| Day 30 | MM 272.8: Deleting the Dead Weight | 59 |
| Day 31 | MM 263.2: Being a Student | 61 |
| Day 32 | MM 304.6: And Then? | 63 |
| Day 33 | MM 296.4: God's Timing, Not Mine | 65 |
| Day 34 | MM 289.8: You Belong Here | 67 |
| Day 35 | MM 293.2: Stop Seeking Validation | 69 |
| Day 36 | MM 303.6: What You're Not Changing | 71 |
| Day 37 | MM 256.2: Celebrate Their Season | 73 |
| Day 38 | MM 292.4: The Weight of No | 75 |
| Day 39 | MM 288.4: The Relationship that Matters | 77 |
| Day 40 | MM 280.6: Built Over Time | 79 |
| Day 41 | MM 290.8: Stop Complaining | 81 |
| Day 42 | MM 259.6: Out of Your Head | 83 |
| Day 43 | MM 282.8: Trust The Process | 85 |
| Day 44 | MM 289.4: The Journey to Key West | 87 |
| Day 45 | MM 268.2: Rejection is Favor | 89 |
| Day 46 | MM 254.8: The Weight of Comparison | 91 |
| Day 47 | MM 252.6: The Risk Worth Taking | 93 |
| Day 48 | MM 302.6: Consistency Builds Character | 95 |

| | | |
|---|---|---|
| **Day 49** | MM 253.6: The Pivot from Pain | 97 |
| **Day 50** | MM 298.6: Embracing Reality | 99 |
| **Day 51** | MM 299.4: The Permission to Be Real | 101 |
| **Day 52** | MM 292.2: Questions You Need To Ask | 103 |
| **Day 53** | MM 271.4: Guard Your Lane | 105 |
| **Day 54** | MM 248.6: The Mirror Never Lies | 107 |
| **Day 55** | MM 251.8: Stand In The Uncomfortable | 109 |
| **Day 56** | MM 252.4: Stop Listening To Them | 111 |
| **Day 57** | MM 284.4: Today is a New Day | 113 |
| **Day 58** | MM 276.4: Allow Life to Be Life | 115 |
| **Day 59** | MM 265.8: The Pruning Season | 117 |
| **Day 60** | MM 289.2: The Power of Silence | 119 |
| **Day 61** | MM 269.4: The Gift of Today | 121 |
| **Day 62** | MM 298.4: The Weight of Perfection | 123 |
| **Day 63** | MM 244.4: The Reset Button | 125 |
| **Day 64** | MM 250.8: The Voices You Listen To | 127 |
| **Day 65** | MM 303.2: Halfway There | 129 |
| **Day 66** | MM 254.6: The Cost of Comfort | 131 |
| **Day 67** | MM 243.8: The Comparison Trap Returns | 133 |
| **Day 68** | MM 278.8: The Power of No | 135 |
| **Day 69** | MM 281.2: The Unseen Work | 137 |
| **Day 70** | MM 258.2: The People Who Stay | 139 |
| **Day 71** | MM 287.6: The Weight of Expectations | 141 |
| **Day 72** | MM 292.6: The Discipline of Waiting | 143 |
| **Day 73** | MM 288.2: The Lesson in the Detour | 145 |
| **Day 74** | MM 290.4: The Gift Of Anonymity | 147 |

| | |
|---|---:|
| **Day 75** \| MM 246.8: The Measure of Success | 149 |
| **Day 76** \| MM 277.4: The Cost of Silence | 151 |
| **Day 77** \| MM 302.8: The Rhythm of Rest | 153 |
| **Day 78** \| MM 249.6: The People You Outgrow | 155 |
| **Day 79** \| MM 285.8: The Mirror You Avoid | 157 |
| **Day 80** \| MM 262.4: The Weight of Unforgiveness | 159 |
| **Day 81** \| MM 301: The Power of Proximity | 161 |
| **Day 82** \| MM 254.2: The Courage to Start Over | 163 |
| **Day 83** \| MM 252.2: The Truth About Momentum | 165 |
| **Day 84** \| MM 304.8: Stop Doubting Yourself | 167 |
| **Day 85** \| MM 304.2: And the Road Ahead | 169 |
| **Day 86** \| MM 271.8: Facing the Mirror | 171 |
| **Day 87** \| MM 282.2: An Act of Service | 173 |
| **Day 88** \| MM 283.6: Elevate Your Brand | 175 |
| **Day 89** \| MM 265.4: The Blessings of Delays | 177 |
| **Day 90** \| MM 272.4: Tomorrow is Not Promised | 179 |
| **Day 91** \| MM 267.8: How Hungry Are You? | 181 |
| **Day 92** \| MM 304.4: The Lesson in the Struggle | 183 |
| **Day 93** \| MM 296.8: The Mirror We Avoid | 185 |
| **Day 94** \| MM 289.6: The Open Door | 187 |
| **Day 95** \| MM 293.4: The Playground of Life | 189 |
| **Day 96** \| MM 259.2: The Mystery of Dreams | 191 |
| **Day 97** \| MM 284.6: You Deserve Better | 193 |
| **Day 98** \| MM 247.8: The Beauty of The Journey | 195 |
| **Day 99** \| MM 241.4: What Will You Create? | 197 |
| **Day 100** \| MM 240.0: Make Yourself Proud | 199 |

| | |
|---|---|
| About the Author | 203 |
| Acknowledgments | 205 |
| Additional Publications | 207 |

# INTRODUCTION

## Mile Marker 00: The Beginning

*I never paid much attention to mile markers until I started commuting every day.*

THE EXPERIENCES OF LIFE, OPENING REFLECTION

I never paid much attention to mile markers until I started commuting every day. Before then, the road was just something to cross, not something to notice. But after years of driving the same stretch of highway, I started to see those small blue signs differently. They sat at the edge of the pavement—steady and unbothered—quietly measuring distance.

The first mile marker I remember noticing was Mile Marker 304, right across from the Milwaukee County Zoo on I-94. That was the beginning of my daily journey. Each morning, as I merged onto the interstate headed toward Madison, that sign seemed to greet me. Along that stretch to Madison and back, every marker stood like a witness to motion, reminding me that progress happens even when it feels slow.

I remember one morning when the light broke through the clouds and brushed the sign ahead in gold. The color of the marker against the sky caught me. Its blue felt calming, constant, and faithful. It didn't demand attention. It simply marked the truth that I was on my way.

A mile marker is a numbered sign placed at intervals along a highway to indicate the distance traveled, typically from a starting point such as a state line. These markers are essential for navigation, helping drivers track their location and plan stops. They also serve as reference points for emergency services and highway maintenance crews to pinpoint exact locations.

That simple definition says a lot about life. We all need markers that tell us where we are, how far we've come, and how close we are to help when things break down. Your personal mile markers are conversations, lessons, and moments of pause that remind you you're still on the road.

I'd seen the highway every season. I'd driven beneath summer skies so bright they made the trees shimmer with life. I'd watched the leaves of fall drift across my windshield like reminders that change is both beautiful and necessary. I'd driven through the silence of winter mornings when the snow covered everything in white, slowing the world long enough for me to think. I'd faced storms that made me pull over, rain pounding so hard that I couldn't see the next sign ahead. In each season, the road taught me something different.

Over time, I began recording what I learned during those drives. Sometimes I spoke on my phone between exits. Other times, I rode in silence, letting my thoughts settle until I reached my destination. For one hundred days, I captured these moments—my personal mile markers. There were times when I was happy and times when I was broken. Moments of laughter that filled the car, and others when tears blurred my vision more than the rain. There were days when God and I had long conversations about life, purpose, and patience. Days when I searched for answers and somehow found comfort in the quiet.

During those drives, I talked with loved ones about their pain and celebrated their victories. I listened to friends share their worries and tried to offer words that might steady them. I also faced myself—my own mistakes, missed turns, and stubborn detours. Each moment became part of a larger story about grace, growth, and becoming. They were all liberating in their own way, pushing me closer to purpose.

What I found was that every day carried a lesson, and every lesson became its own mile marker. These reflections formed a map, a record of what the road revealed and how faith kept me moving forward.

Mile Markers 304 through 240 are the result of that journey. Each devotion holds a piece of the highway: a story, a reflection, a truth about motion and meaning. Some will meet you in joy. Others may meet you in grief. But each one is designed to remind you that even in waiting, you are still progressing.

The beauty of a mile marker is that it doesn't just show distance; it confirms direction. It stands as quiet proof that movement continues, even when you can't see the destination.

So here you are, at Mile Marker 00. Let the journey begin.

# 100 DAYS

# DAY 01

## Mile Marker 304: Traveling Tires

*"Life will present moments that shock our reality, and we have to decide to keep going or pull over to the side of the road and give up."*

KEYIMANI ALFORD

I had just started making regular drives between Milwaukee and Madison. A job landed me in Madison, and I was excited about the opportunity. However, my friends, family, and church remained in Milwaukee, so I was on the road several times a week.

Winter was setting in. Frost rested on the fields. Temperatures dropped fast. I lived in an apartment right off the interstate, which made getting on and off the highway easy, but the complex sat on a steep hill. Madison used more sand than salt, and that morning the ice did not melt the way I hoped.

In the spring, I decided to buy an old truck, a 1997 Ford Bronco. I was proud of that old Ford Bronco because I spent some time fixing it up. Fresh paint. New interior. Twenty-four inch black and burgundy rims. It was quite the project. The day before, I eased down the hill and the Bronco slid. The right rim kissed the curb hard enough to jolt me. I felt it, but I kept moving. The next day I headed to Milwaukee like usual.

I passed Lake Mills and felt a shake in the front tire, but I kept going. As I approached the Johnson Creek exit and crossed the Crawfish River, everything changed. At seventy miles per hour, the right front dropped. The tire popped off and shot forward, bouncing toward the shoulder. I watched it roll past me while I held the wheel tight and kept the Bronco steady. There was a car riding in the lane right beside me. The tire missed that car, hit the curb, jumped the ditch, and disappeared into the field. I guided the Bronco to the shoulder. Three wheels on the ground. My heart was pounding, but my hands stayed steady.

I stepped out and saw it for what it was. That tire was gone. My truck could have flipped. I could have spun into the median. I could have slid into oncoming traffic. Instead, I was standing on the shoulder, alive. I was near the Rock River rest area, and all I could feel was gratitude. I made two calls: one to the towing company and the other to my friend, Schunn. He was always available when I needed him, whether it was driving me out of town for a fraternity trip or, in this case, picking me up from the side of the road to take me back to Milwaukee. The tow truck came and picked up the Bronco, which sat in the garage in Milwaukee until I replaced the tire. That drive became a mile marker I will never forget.

I looked back on it and understood something simple. Life will hand you these kinds of moments. Moments when the day you planned gets interrupted. When the route you know throws you a curve ball. You do not have to like it, but you do have to respond to it. That morning reminded me to be thankful for protection I could see and protection I could not. It also reminded me that inconvenience can be mercy in disguise.

In retrospect, I realize that protection often looks like disruption. It pulls you away from something you might be enjoying, yet grace keeps you steady when life or a wheel comes off unexpectedly. The irony of it all is that God has a unique way of making sure someone is on standby to help you through it all, and in that moment, it was my friend, Schunn.

I now understand that when the unexpected shows up, I must slow down, name what I can handle, let go of what I cannot, and rely on those who were divinely sent to support us along the journey. These days, I choose safety over speed and let the delay teach me instead of letting it define me.

Now let me ask you: Where did your plans wobble this week? Was there an interruption that might have kept you from something worse? What one small step can you take today to adjust your route without losing your peace? And who is in your corner to ensure that you still get to your destination?

***The journey always has something beautiful along the way.***

# DAY 02

## Mile Marker 287.4: Spared

*The LORD will keep you from all harm—he will watch over your life.*
PSALM 121:7 (NIV)

Driving home was always an adventure. Frequently, I'd witness headlights tracing the curve of the highway as dusk settled in. The road was familiar, one I had taken countless times, but it carried its own personality depending on the season. Some evenings felt peaceful, the kind where the sky melted into shades of orange and lavender before fading to night. Other evenings carried a heaviness, like the air itself was whispering to pay attention.

This night felt different. The temperatures had started to drop, pulling away from summer's warmth into fall's early chill. The scent of damp leaves lingered through the vents, and the fields along the highway looked muted, the tall grass bowing in the wind. I noticed the hunting stands near the tree lines, small wooden towers standing guard, silent reminders that the seasons were changing. Around this time of year, deer would start crossing the highway without warning, and dusk became a warning sign to stay alert. It was the hour when anything could happen.

As I drove, I thought about how many times I had been spared on this same stretch of pavement. The near misses. The close calls. The accidents that sometimes unfolded before me. Each memory carried its own pulse. I thought about the cars I'd seen in ditches during winter storms and the flashing lights that filled the sky after a crash. I never wanted to be in that moment. Then I thought about all the times I arrived home safely and never stopped to consider what didn't happen.

Somewhere between exits, gratitude began to rise in me. It wasn't loud or dramatic. It was quiet, steady, and almost reverent. I realized how easily we take safety for granted and how rarely we pause to thank God for what didn't go wrong.

The truth is, we don't always know what we've been spared from. We complain about delays and grow impatient when traffic slows us down. But sometimes those very interruptions are protection. The slowdowns we resist might be the very things saving us from what we will never see. That night reminded me that life is fragile, and grace often works behind the scenes. Gratitude isn't just for the visible blessings. It's for the unseen ones too.

That drive became a mile marker for me. It taught me that every safe arrival, every ordinary commute, every uneventful day is a quiet testimony of grace. Even when we can't see it, something, or Someone, is holding us steady. Gratitude deepens when we notice what could have been but wasn't.

Maybe this is your reminder to slow down. To see delays differently. To whisper thanks for the mercies that never made the headlines of your day.

***Gratitude begins when you notice what God spared you from.***

# DAY 03

## Mile Marker 301.8: Trust

*Trust in the LORD with all your heart and lean not on your own understanding.*

PROVERBS 3:5 (NIV)

Have you ever experienced a morning where the air felt cool and the light still carried a hint of sleep? That was the kind of morning I had. Except I was sitting at the stoplight, waiting to merge onto the interstate during it. The overpass stretched above me, its lines of concrete and steel catching the pale light of dawn. For a moment, I looked up.

I wasn't moving yet—just waiting. The hum of engines surrounded me, the faint echo of traffic overhead filling the stillness. I noticed how weathered the bridge looked in that morning light. The concrete had aged into a dull gray, the kind that tells stories of rain, snow, and heat. Cracks ran across its surface, like veins, and in some places, the edges had chipped away, leaving shadows that deepened with the rising sun. The metal beams that held it all together were rusted in spots, their paint faded and peeling. A few carried graffiti, names, and colors layered over time, telling their own stories of presence and passing.

It wasn't pretty. But it was honest—strong, steady, worn, and real. As I sat there, I thought about how much we trust without ever realizing it. I trusted that the road above would hold. I trusted the concrete and steel to do exactly what they were built to do, even though they looked tired and imperfect. I didn't question it. I didn't analyze it. I simply believed it would hold.

That thought stayed with me. How often do we live this way without noticing it? You sit in chairs without checking their legs. You cross bridges without testing their strength. You lean into routines, trusting that things will work the way they always have. Yet when it comes to trusting God, or even trusting the process of your own growth, you hesitate. You ask if it's safe. You question if the foundation will hold.

That quiet moment before getting on the freeway reminds you that trust isn't something you learn once. It's something you practice every day. The issue isn't whether you know how to trust; it's where you decide to place it. If I could sit beneath tons of concrete and steel without fear, you can surely rest in the hands of a faithful God.

Trust, I've learned, is less about certainty and more about surrender. If I could trust a freeway to hold, you can trust the One who holds you.

***If I can trust a freeway to hold, I can trust the One who holds me.***

# DAY 04

## Mile Marker 261.2: Silence

*Be still and know that I am God.*

PSALM 46:10 (NIV)

It was evening, and I was on my way home. The road stretched out ahead of me, quiet and almost empty—the kind of quiet that makes you more aware of your own thoughts. I didn't turn on the radio. I just drove. The hum of the tires filled the silence as the sky began to fade from orange to gray. It had been a long day, one of those days when I showed up for everyone else but had nothing left for myself.

The silence felt heavy at first, but familiar. There was a time in my life when silence was my only companion. I used to show up in rooms with a smile, doing my best to appear fine, while inside I carried battles no one could see. My laughter worked like a disguise, covering the noise I couldn't explain. Those memories came rushing back as the road carried me forward.

The more I drove, the more I realized how much silence had taught me. It slowed me when I wanted to rush. It made me think when I wanted to avoid. It brought me face-to-face with the things I tried to bury beneath busyness. Silence wouldn't let me skip the lessons I needed to learn, and though it was uncomfortable, it was sacred in its own way.

We often treat silence like an enemy, but maybe it's a teacher. When was the last time you sat in stillness without trying to fix something, distract yourself, or rush to the next thing? Sometimes silence reveals the truth you've been too busy to hear. One strategy I've adopted in meetings is to let silence create space for people to reflect and think. I'll admit, it can feel awkward, but it almost always invites someone to step up and share their perspective. We need similar moments in our own lives, where the awkward quiet gives us room to sit with our thoughts and produce something meaningful.

Looking back, I see that silence built something in me that words couldn't. It strengthened my patience. It gave me the courage to sit with my own thoughts.

It showed me that strength isn't always seen or heard. It is often developed in quiet places, on drives like this one, when the world doesn't demand performance, only presence.

The lessons I gained in silence became the strength I carried when it was time to speak.

*Some of life's greatest answers will be provided when no one else is talking.*

# DAY 05

## Mile Marker 300.4: Shifting Circles

*"There is a time for everything, and a season for every activity under the heavens."*
ECCLESIASTES 3:1 (NIV)

Early morning drives when the air is cool and the sun begins to stretch across the horizon, brings me such joy. It feels just as good when the road is open and the city is quiet because there is no traffic. These are the kind of drives when I think the most: no music, no distractions, just me and my thoughts moving with the car. That morning, my mind wandered to the people in my life and how much that circle had changed over the years.

There are times in life when the people you thought would always be close to you begin to drift. I used to take it personally. I would sit and wonder what I did wrong or replay conversations in my head, searching for the reason why the relationship felt different. But the older I get, the more I realize that distance doesn't always mean rejection. Sometimes it's God's way of reshaping your circle. Sometimes it's life creating space for the next chapter you're meant to walk into.

I remember a season when I was stepping into new opportunities and trying to stay focused on where I was headed. During that time, some of the relationships I counted on the most began to shift. At first, it hurt. I questioned myself and the choices I was making. But eventually, I realized those relationships had run their course. The truth is, not everyone can go with you into every season of life. Some people are only assigned to you for a chapter, not the whole story.

If you've ever felt that distance—when someone steps back and you don't understand why—try not to rush to fill the space. Sometimes the silence between you and another person isn't punishment; it's preparation. It's clearing room for growth. It's making way for what's next.

That shift taught me to stop panicking when people stepped back. Instead, I began to see it as a sign that something new is forming. I have to accept that the circle around me might not look the same tomorrow as it did yesterday, and that's okay. Because the right people—the ones meant for your journey—will always meet you in the right season.

Sometimes the empty space around you is the very thing building the strength inside you.

*Not everyone is meant for every season.*
*Trust who stays and release who leaves.*

# DAY 06

## Mile Marker 249.2: Peace in Chaos

*"Peace I leave with you; my peace I give you. I do not give to you as the world gives. Do not let your hearts be troubled and do not be afraid."*

JOHN 14:27 (NIV)

Peace was something I searched for, sometimes in the smallest moments. One familiar sight on my drives was crossing the Rock and Crawfish Rivers on I-94. They were unpredictable. During rainy seasons, they would swell beyond their banks, flooding the fields that surrounded them. The water would stretch wide, covering fences, swallowing patches of grass, and creeping toward the road.

When the rains stopped, the rivers would slowly pull back into their place, leaving behind dark, rich soil that shimmered in the sunlight. New patches of green would appear where water once sat, and life quietly returned to the land. There was something powerful about that rhythm. I always admired it. Every time I crossed those bridges, I'd find myself glancing over, caught between curiosity and peace. Maybe I wanted to see if a fish would jump, or maybe I was drawn to how calm the river looked, even after all its chaos.

It reminded me that life works the same way. There are seasons when everything feels out of control, when problems flood in and you can't see the edges anymore. It's messy and unpredictable. The weight of it all can cover your plans, your focus, even your joy. But like the rivers, the chaos doesn't last forever.

The water eventually recedes. The land breathes again. What once looked like destruction becomes fertile ground.

Maybe you're in a flooded season right now, where everything feels submerged and uncertain. It might seem like you'll never recover from what's overflowed. But trust this: every flood crests eventually. The same waters that overwhelm you now can be the same ones that bring new life later.

Each time I cross those bridges, I'm reminded that peace isn't found in avoiding the flood. It's found in knowing that when it rises, it will also fall, and life will grow again where the water once stood.

*Peace comes from knowing the flood will recede and life will grow again.*

# DAY 07

## Mile Marker 268.4: The Gift of Consistency

*"Let us not become weary in doing good, for at the proper time we will reap a harvest if we do not give up."*

GALATIANS 6:9 (NIV)

The morning felt heavier than usual. The sky was still waking up, streaks of soft gray stretching over the horizon. I was driving to work, coffee in hand, moving slower than I wanted to admit. It was one of those mornings when motivation felt miles away. The kind of morning when the road felt longer, the air felt thicker, and the to-do list waiting ahead felt like too much.

I've learned that consistency has been one of the hardest lessons for me to master. But it has also been one of the most rewarding. Over time, I realized that consistency isn't about being perfect. It isn't about doing everything right all the time. It is about showing up. Even when you are tired. Even when no one notices. Even when progress feels invisible.

There were plenty of mornings when I didn't feel like pushing myself. It would have been easy to hit snooze, roll over, and tell myself that tomorrow would be better. But the truth is, tomorrow often turned into another tomorrow, and then another. Before I knew it, I had convinced myself that waiting was wisdom when it was really avoidance.

The road hummed beneath my tires as I thought about how many seasons I had been through when quitting would have been the easy choice. Seasons when the work didn't seem worth it, when results came too slow, and when I wondered if my efforts were even making a difference. But I kept showing up. Looking back, I see now that those quiet seasons were never wasted. They were training ground. Every small step, every tiring day, every moment I chose discipline over comfort was preparing me for what was next.

Maybe you are in one of those quiet seasons, too, the kind that makes you question if your efforts matter. Can I tell you something? They do. What feels slow today is building the kind of strength that does not fade when the spotlight dims. Consistency does not always give you fast results, but it gives you lasting ones.

That is worth the wait, and it is worth the weight.

***Consistency builds character when no one is watching and rewards when everyone sees.**

# DAY 08

## Mile Marker 254.4: Small Joys

*"This is the day the LORD has made; let us rejoice and be glad in it."*
PSALM 118:24 (NIV)

It was a long day, the kind that drained more energy than I wanted to give. I was driving as the sun began to set. Usually, the orange glow stretched across the sky like a soft curtain, drawing the day to a close. This time it didn't. The sky was gray and tired, mirroring how I felt. It gave the kind of "I'm over it" vibe that sometimes settles in after a day that's been too much. Still, the road was quiet, and for a while, so was I. That silence gave me time to think and reflect.

Life has a way of overwhelming us. We want big solutions for big problems. We want the one thing that will fix everything. But life doesn't usually work like that. I've learned that the strength to keep going doesn't always come from one big answer. Sometimes it comes from the small joys scattered along the way.

For me, it's often simple things. A piece of candy waiting in the console. A quiet fishing trip on a Saturday morning. Watching a movie I've already seen a dozen times. Those small things don't erase the challenges I face, but they remind me that joy still exists in the middle of them. They give me just enough strength to keep moving when my spirit feels heavy.

As I passed Lake Mills, the moon reflected what little light was left behind the clouds. It wasn't as bright as usual, but it still shimmered enough to catch my attention. That small moment felt like a whisper from God, reminding me that even on weary days, light still finds a way through.

Maybe you've been searching for one big breakthrough to make everything better. But what if what you need most is already around you, hidden in the quiet details you keep passing by? The laugh you share with someone you love. The song that hits you just right. The warmth of a good meal after a long day.

Small joys are not distractions from life's struggles. They are reminders that even in hard seasons, God still leaves pieces of goodness to hold onto. Joy isn't always loud or dramatic. Sometimes it's found in the stillness, tucked into the small moments that remind you that life is still good.

***Small joys are God's reminders that even in struggle, goodness remains.***

# DAY 09

## Mile Marker 302.2: Endurance

*"Blessed is the one who perseveres under trial because, having stood the test, that person will receive the crown of life that the Lord has promised to those who love him."*

JAMES 1:12 (NIV)

Endurance is a word we don't celebrate enough. We love the sound of victory. We love the stories of breakthroughs. But endurance often looks like quiet faithfulness when no one is cheering.

It was one of those cold mornings when you could see your breath in the air—the kind that makes you turn up the heat a little higher just to get comfortable. It was also one of those mornings when I honestly didn't want to be on the highway driving to work. Winter driving always tested me: slower traffic, unpredictable ice patches, and a chill that seeped into my bones. It was a season that forced me to be patient and cautious, no matter how much I wanted to rush ahead.

That morning, the highway streaked with lines of salt from the snow the night before. I was tired, not just from the morning but from the week, yet I pressed my way anyhow.

I've learned that endurance isn't about speed. It's about strength. It's staying in the race when your legs feel heavy. It's breathing through the weight of the moment and believing you'll see the finish line if you just keep moving.

There were seasons when I wanted to quit. There were moments when I felt the journey from Milwaukee to Madison wasn't worth it. It always seemed to happen in winter, when conditions weren't the best and it took a little more time to get going. And I must be honest, being a California baby, Wisconsin winters always made me question why I lived here. Those days only amplified those thoughts. They reminded me of seasons when responsibilities felt endless, losses cut deep, and setbacks kept stacking up.

But every time I endured and made the decision to just do it—to make that drive—something shifted. I discovered new strength waiting on the other side.

Maybe it was a smile from a colleague, an unexpected conversation that made my day, or a moment when I was simply productive.

It would never have revealed itself if I hadn't endured. That was a form of growth. On this drive, life reminded me that winning isn't always about being first. Sometimes it's about not giving up and bearing the road ahead.

If you're tired right now, don't discount what endurance is building in you. The strength you're gaining today might be the same strength you'll need tomorrow.

***Endurance doesn't rush you to the finish line.***
***It builds the strength to carry you there.***

# DAY 10

## Mile Marker 292.8: Letting Go

*"Cast all your anxiety on him because he cares for you."*
1 PETER 5:7 (NIV)

I pulled out onto the highway with a venti white chocolate mocha sitting in the cup holder beside me from Starbucks right down the street. The first few sips always helped me settle into the day and regulate my early morning commute. Traffic was light, and the rhythm of the tires against the pavement left space for my thoughts to wander.

Lately, I had been wrestling with things I couldn't control—plans that didn't work out, conversations that didn't go the way I hoped, and outcomes that refused to fit into my timeline.

One of the hardest lessons I had to face was letting go of control. I liked to have plans. I liked knowing what was coming next. But life didn't always move according to what I expected. And that was hard to accept.

There were times when I fought to hold on to things that were no longer meant for me—relationships, jobs, opportunities. I thought control would give me peace, but instead, it left me drained. The tighter I tried to hold, the more anxious I became.

It wasn't until I loosened my grip and trusted God with the outcome that I finally found the peace I'd been chasing. Letting go didn't mean I stopped caring or trying. It meant I started believing that what's ahead is greater than what I'm holding on to.

As I passed the stretch of open field near Johnson Creek, my eyes drifted toward the hill where the trash was collected, rising up on the side of the highway. At the bottom of that hill sat a small pond with old trees leaning over the water, their branches worn and twisted from years of weather. If you looked closely, you could see bird nests tucked into those branches, resting there like quiet homes. It was the perfect habitat, tucked right off the highway where most people passed by without noticing.

Above all, a few hawks glided in slow circles, steady and unbothered by the wind. There was usually a small group of them, riding in the air together. They didn't flap around in panic or fight for control. They let the air carry them. Watching them, I was reminded that peace often begins when we stop forcing outcomes and start trusting the process.

If you're tired from trying to hold everything together, take a breath. Surrender what's weighing you down. You were never meant to carry it all alone. When you do, you'll realize that life is so much easier to carry.

Why? Well, because letting go isn't giving up. It's trusting that God has something better waiting ahead. And trusting His plan is always easier than carrying our own.

***Letting go isn't giving up. It's trusting that God has something better waiting ahead.***

# DAY 11

## Mile Marker 286.6: Perspective Shift

*"In all things God works for the good of those who love him, who have been called according to his purpose."*

ROMANS 8:28 (NIV)

Somewhere between Sullivan and Johnson Creek, it happened. A traffic jam. All vehicles had come to a complete stop—the kind of standstill where you know something serious is ahead. Cars were stacked in every lane, brake lights glowing against the gray of the day. There was no exit nearby and no way to turn around. We were all just there, waiting.

People started shifting in their seats, looking at their watches, honking out of frustration. I remember glancing at the clock too, realizing how long I'd already been sitting still. But somewhere in the middle of all that noise, my mind started to quiet. I thought about how many times I had driven that same road without a second thought. Mile after mile, it had always been routine. But that day, something broke the pattern.

It made me realize how quickly life can change. We move through our days, assuming things will always stay the same. Same route. Same rhythm. Same routine. But all it takes is one unexpected moment to remind us how fragile life really is. What feels ordinary today can shift in an instant.

How many times have you found yourself trying to rush life because something altered your plans? Maybe the kids took longer than usual to get dressed. Maybe the McDonald's drive-thru was busier than normal. Or maybe it was those red lights that always seemed to catch you at the wrong moment. Either way, that pause—that delay—might have been there for a specific reason.

Sitting there on the freeway, I stopped thinking about when traffic would move again. I started thinking about the blessing of all the times it had. The times I had made it home safely. The mornings when the roads were clear. The hundreds of uneventful commutes that quietly carried me without interruption.

Cars were all around me, a picture of the many responsibilities and distractions that press in on us every day. In that moment, I realized the pause was not just about waiting in traffic. It was about perspective. It reminded me that even the routines I often take for granted are small miracles in disguise.

***What feels ordinary today is often the blessing you'll remember tomorrow.***

# DAY 12

## Mile Marker 300.2: Familiar Roads, New Lessons

*"Show me your ways, LORD, teach me your paths."*
PSALM 25:4 (NIV)

Late in the afternoon, I found myself driving down a road I had traveled hundreds of times before. Same exits. Same turns. Same scenery. For years, I passed that way without thinking twice. It had become routine, a straight line between where I was and where I needed to be.

But that day, something caught my attention, a building I had never really noticed before. A tall oak standing firm near Pewaukee, its leaves just beginning to shift color. Even the way the sunlight hit the curve of the road looked different. It stopped me in thought. How many times have I passed this exact spot and never really seen it?

That drive reminded me how easy it is to live on autopilot. We rush through our routines, same schedule, same faces, same plans, barely paying attention to the details right in front of us. In doing so, we miss the small reminders of beauty, growth, and God's presence woven into our everyday lives.

Autopilot does not only show up in how we drive. It shows up in how we speak, how we pray, and how we respond to the people closest to us. We can start repeating the same phrases, giving the same answers, showing up the same way, without ever checking in with our own heart. After a while, we are present in body but absent in spirit. Life starts to feel like a blur of tasks instead of a journey of moments.

What if God is using these familiar routes to whisper something we have been too busy to hear? A nudge to forgive. A reminder to rest. A quiet invitation to see ourselves and others with fresh eyes. The road does not change, but our awareness can. That day, as I noticed the oak tree and the light across the pavement, I sensed God saying, "You have been here before, but you have not seen it like this." And I realized, sometimes that is all it takes, a small shift in attention that turns a regular drive into a conversation with God.

Very often, the only difference between routine and revelation is the pace we choose. When we slow down just enough to breathe, notice, and listen, the ordinary moments of our day begins to carry meaning. My awareness came around Mile Marker 300.2, and in that moment, I promised myself I'd pay a little closer attention to things like a coworker's expression, a child's question, or even a sunrise I usually ignore. All of these become mile markers that remind us that God is closer than we think, even on the roads we feel we know by heart.

That day, the familiar road taught me that just because something is ordinary does not mean it has nothing to show us. Sometimes the lessons, the reminders, and the inspiration we need are hidden in the very places we overlook. All it takes is a shift in perspective, a willingness to slow down, to pay attention, and to open our eyes to what has always been there.

***Familiar roads still have new lessons if we're willing to pay attention.***

# DAY 13

## Mile Marker 245.4: The Power of Stillness

*"The LORD will fight for you; you need only to be still."*
EXODUS 14:14 (NIV)

An hour on the road might feel like wasted time to some people, but for me, it has become one of the most important spaces in my life. No meetings. No constant noise. Just me, the open highway, and the thoughts that rise when the world finally gets quiet.

When I originally moved back to Milwaukee from Madison, the drive was one thing I felt increased apprehension about. I'd put more miles on my car. I'd have to drive during the wintertime. And most importantly, I'd be making this drive alone—every single day.

Then I realized something when it started. The drive to work had become one of the few parts of my day where life slowed down.

That day, the highway stretched open ahead of me, the light just starting to rise over the fields near Delafield. Being a brisk morning, I had the heat on to warm me up, and for once, I didn't reach for the radio to turn up the noise. I just let silence fill the space.

In that silence, I wrestled with questions I didn't want to ask out loud. I replayed hard conversations. I celebrated quiet victories. I sat with God—not always with words, but with openness. And more often than not, that silence spoke back to me. Not in some booming voice, but in clarity. In perspective. In peace, I didn't realize I needed.

In these same kinds of moments in the past, I've gotten answers to questions, guidance for next steps, bold ideas to write books, and assurance that I was on the right path. These mile markers, as I call them, have become transformational.

Have you ever sat in silence with expectation? Without interruption? With a moment that simply demanded your attention?

What I've come to understand is that silence isn't empty. Silence is full. It gives room for reflection. It makes space for lessons that keeps us from seeing. It reminds you that stillness is not wasted time. It's preparation.

Those drives taught me that silence is a teacher if you're willing to listen. It doesn't erase the noise of life, but it gives you a different way to face it. And sometimes the greatest strength comes not from the words we speak, but from the stillness we allow ourselves to sit in.

***Silence is not empty. It is full of lessons busyness tries to hide.***

# DAY 14

## Mile Marker 260.4: The Cost of Sacrifice

*"For where your treasure is, there your heart will be also."*
MATTHEW 6:21 (NIV)

Often, my deepest and most intense thinking happens in the morning—on those journeys to work when the day is beginning, but life keeps moving on. This morning was no different when the thought hit me: how much sacrifice really costs.

My drive is sometimes quiet, the kind where your mind drifts between what's ahead and what you've left behind. This time it wasn't. I was listening to one of my favorite gospel artists, Lisa Page-Brooks, thinking about what she had to sacrifice when her husband passed—a life she was accustomed to, a partnership she adored, the protection of a life partner, a provider, protector, and defender.

Then I began to think about the many things I'd had to give up through the years. Some of them are small. Others that required real surrender. These were the kinds of things that ran through my mind on these drives.

Sacrifice can feel like loss in the moment—giving up time, resources, even pieces of comfort you'd rather hold on to. But over time, I've learned that sacrifice isn't wasted. It's an investment.

There were seasons when I sacrificed my own plans to support family. Times when I gave up sleep to chase a goal. Times when I set aside what I wanted in the moment for the sake of something greater later. And in every one of those seasons, I didn't always see the blessing right away. But looking back now, I can see it clearly.

Sacrifice taught me that real growth often requires letting go. It stretched me in ways that comfort never could. It shaped my priorities and helped me see what truly matters. And it reminded me that while sacrifice hurts, it also builds strength and character.

Maybe you're in a season of sacrifice too—giving your all and wondering if it will ever pay off. Hold steady. The truth is nothing worth building comes without it. Whether it's your dreams, your relationships, or your faith, the blessing often hides on the other side of what you're willing to give up.

***Sacrifice isn't loss. It's the seed that grows blessing.*愛**

# DAY 15

## Mile Marker 269.8: Learning to Pivot

*"In their hearts humans plan their course, but the LORD establishes their steps."*

PROVERBS 16:9 (NIV)

It was one of those drives where life seemed to change all at once—the light, the traffic, even my direction. I was headed home after a long day at work, one of those nights when I just wanted the road to be smooth and quiet. But as I got closer to Cottage Grove, I noticed the orange glow of construction lights flickering in the distance.

Crews were repaving the highway, the truck easing forward as workers placed orange cones one by one, closing off lanes and slowing everything down. The smell of hot asphalt filled the air, and the rhythm of progress came at a crawl. I sighed, knowing this stretch of the highway was about to test my patience again.

After what felt like forever, I finally passed the construction zone, only to see flashing lights ahead. From a distance, I could see the red and blue strobes of sheriff's vehicles cutting through the night sky. As I approached, their headlights reflected off the cones, forming a wall of light that forced traffic to a stop. The officers were diverting cars off the highway, guiding everyone onto a back-road detour. I didn't know why. I just followed the new path.

As I drove through the dark back roads, I thought about how much life feels like that sometimes. You think you've mapped out every turn, every stop, every next step, and then something shifts. A job changes. A relationship ends. A plan falls through. For a long time, I struggled with that. I thought pivots meant failure.

But over time, I realized pivots are proof that you're still moving. They're the adjustments that keep you aligned when the original path no longer fits. Some of my best opportunities came after I pivoted. Some of my most meaningful lessons showed up when I thought the road had ended, only to discover there was a new lane waiting.

Pivoting taught me flexibility. It taught me to trust that even when my plans break, the journey doesn't end. And most importantly, it showed me that God's direction is bigger than my map.

Maybe you've found yourself in that same place, trying to make sense of a change you didn't choose. Don't fight it too hard. Sometimes what feels like a disruption is really a divine redirection.

I've learned to lean into those moments now, because a pivot might just be the turn that leads me closer to purpose.

***A pivot isn't failure. It's proof you're still moving towards purpose.***

# DAY 16

## Mile Marker 247.2: Finding Focus

*"Be careful for nothing; but in everything by prayer and supplication with thanksgiving let your requests be made known unto God. And the peace of God, which passeth all understanding, shall keep your hearts and minds through Christ Jesus."*

PHILIPPIANS 4:6-7 (KJV)

Long days at work make me want to get home fast, but sometimes the journey on the road can be a blessing or a curse. Being in my thoughts wasn't always the best thing, especially when there was a lot before me.

In that moment, I was in my car and on the road when I started thinking about an opportunity that would unfold over the next nine months. The highway was calm, yet my thoughts weren't. Preparing for what was ahead made me reflect deeply on who I am, what I want to accomplish, and the kind of impact I hope to leave in my profession and in the world.

The truth is, ideas flood me daily. Books I want to write. Businesses I want to start. Career moves I still hope to make. It sometimes felt like I was racing against time, and part of that urgency came from knowing how short life can be. I'm 46 now, and as a Black man, I recognize tomorrow is never promised. That thought drives me, but it also pressures me.

Balancing that tension hasn't been easy. On one hand, I want to chase every idea at once. On the other, I know that rushing to do everything often leaves you with nothing finished. That's where I've been living lately, in the tension between desire and discipline. It's teaching me something important: focus.

Focus isn't about ignoring your dreams. It's about trusting that not everything needs to happen today. It's pacing yourself, honoring the process, and realizing that what's meant for you will meet you in time.

In higher education, I see this every day. Demands pile up, and priorities fight for attention. But not everything is urgent. Some things can wait. Some things require prayer, patience, and a clear sense of capacity.

That's what Philippians reminds you. Peace doesn't come from finishing everything. It comes from releasing what you can't control. I'm learning that when I surrender my anxious striving and trust God with the pace of my purpose, peace finds me, even on the busiest highway.

***Focus isn't doing everything.***
***It's trusting that what's meant for you will come in time.***

# DAY 17

## Mile Marker 263.6: Shattered Glass

*"The LORD is close to the brokenhearted and saves those who are crushed in spirit."*
PSALM 34:18 (NIV)

The brake lights ahead came on suddenly. I eased off the gas and felt the car slow beneath me. Traffic was backing up fast, which was unusual for this time of morning. I checked the clock on the dashboard. I had time, but not much. My mind started calculating how long this delay would cost me.

Then I saw the flashing lights.

Red and blue streaked across the gray morning sky. A sheriff's vehicle was weaving through the stopped cars, trying to reach whatever had happened up ahead. I watched drivers shift their vehicles, making space where there seemed to be none. Slowly, the path opened, and the officer moved through.

As I inched forward, I could see the wreckage. Glass covered the road like scattered stars. A car sat crumpled on the shoulder, its front end smashed, airbags deflated and hanging lifeless—the kind of accident that makes you hold your breath, the kind that reminds you how fast everything can change.

But then I saw him—a young man standing on the side of the road, talking to an officer. He was whole. He was walking. He was alive.

I exhaled.

My frustration about the delay melted into something else: gratitude, relief, a deep awareness that this could have been me. How many mornings had I driven this same road without incident? How many times had I arrived at work safely and never stopped to thank God for the trip?

We ask for so much. We pray for blessings and breakthroughs. We want promotions and provisions. But how often do you thank God for what didn't happen—for the accidents that missed you, for the dangers you never saw because He moved them out of your path?

The traffic started moving again. I passed the wreckage slowly, carefully. That young man was still standing there—shaken, but safe—protected by something greater than luck.

As I merged back into the flow of the highway, I whispered a prayer: Thank You, God. Not for more. Not for better. Just thanks. Thanks for every uneventful drive. Thanks for every safe arrival. Thanks for the mornings I woke up healthy and whole.

Sometimes God's greatest work isn't in what He gives us. It's in what He shields us from.

*The best blessings are seeing them seen on others around you.*

# DAY 18

## Mile Marker 248.8: The Yacht on My Screen

*"Now to him who is able to do immeasurably more than all we ask or imagine, according to his power that is at work within us."*

EPHESIANS 3:20 (NIV)

I was sitting at a red light, waiting for my turn to merge onto the freeway, when I pulled out my phone and started scrolling. I knew I shouldn't have, but the light was long, and my mind was already wandering. That's when I saw it. A video of the rapper, Ludacris, on a yacht, running on a treadmill in the middle of the ocean off the coast of Italy. The water behind him was impossibly blue. The sun painted everything gold. He looked free. Unbothered. Living.

My first thought hit fast: "Man, I wish I could do that." But then the light changed. I put the phone down, pressed the gas, and merged onto I-94. The highway stretched out in front of me, familiar and predictable. And as I settled into the drive, something shifted in me.

A different thought rose up. A better one. What if I wasn't supposed to envy what I saw? What if I was supposed to be inspired by it? I thought about that video again, but this time without the sting of comparison.

Ludacris wasn't on that yacht to make me feel small. He was there to show me what's possible. His success wasn't my loss. It was my window into what God can do.

You do this all the time. You see people thriving and immediately feel less than. You measure your progress against theirs and come up short every single time. But what if you shift your perspective? What if, instead of wanting what they have, you see them as proof of what's available?

Scripture says God is able to do exceedingly, abundantly above all that we ask or think. That means His plans for you are bigger than your imagination. The blessings He has in store aren't capped by what feels reasonable.

I passed Mile Marker 248.8 and smiled. Every day, I drove to a job I was grateful for. But what if God wants to give you a lifestyle where you're also on a yacht somewhere, living fully, inspiring others, walking in the overflow He promised? That's not greed. That's faith.

So, when you see someone else winning, don't get discouraged. Get inspired. Let it fuel you. Let it remind you that God is still in the business of opening doors you didn't even know existed.

*Someone else's blessing is proof of what God can do, not a limit on what He won't do for us.*

# DAY 19

## Mile Marker 259.8: Know Your Worth

*"The Lord makes firm the steps of the one who delights in him."*
PSALM 37:23 (NIV)

This morning was peculiar. I usually wake up at 6:00 a.m., but today I opened my eyes at 4:30 a.m., already thinking through the day, the drive to Madison, and the list I needed to accomplish. As I lay there, a quiet question dropped in my spirit: "What is your worth?"

That question took me back to a recent trip. I had just returned from a national conference that brings together colleges and universities from across the country to talk about serving students, especially those from underrepresented backgrounds. It was a full schedule. Over a few days, I traveled between cities, carried four different assignments, and poured into leaders who care deeply about student success.

Two weeks before going, I was offered something that looked like a great opportunity. Another session. Another space to teach. Another room full of people. On the surface, it sounded good. But as I listened more closely, I realized it would require a heavy investment with no real investment back into me. New materials. New insights. Interactive exercises for hundreds of people. Tight preparation time. High expectations. Yet no value attached to the work.

I said no.

I did not say no because I am afraid of work. I said no because sometimes an invitation is really a withdrawal. It pulls from your time, your energy, and your creativity, but offers no honor, support, or recognition in return. Saying yes would have meant stretching myself even thinner in a season when my plate was already full.

Walking those conference halls later, hearing the buzz of sessions and conversations, I thought about the opportunity I turned down. Part of me wondered what it might have led to. But as I talked with a colleague, something settled in my heart. Sometimes you must walk away when a person or organization does not value your worth. Saying no protected my peace, my name, and the standard God gave me for the work I do.

That is what I was thinking about on the highway this morning. I passed signs for Milwaukee, Madison, and Beloit, each one pointing to different lanes and different destinations. Somewhere around Mile Marker 259.8, it clicked. Life is like that stretch of road. You get options: east, west, north, or south. Many paths look open, but not every path is for you. In those moments, you have to ask, "What destination am I really headed toward?" That clarity reassured me that I had made the right decision. Opportunities that diminish your value are not really opportunities. They are detours.

The truth is many of us have learned to measure our worth by how much we say yes. We tie our value to how many people ask for our help, invite us to the table, or need our skills. Being in demand can feel flattering, but if we are not careful, we confuse being busy with being aligned. We end up tired, overcommitted, and quietly frustrated, all while calling it "purpose."

You may be in a moment where you have to think carefully about alignment and ask, "Does this fit my assignment, or does it feed my ego?" That is not an easy question, but it is an honest one. Some invitations look impressive from the outside, yet under the surface they add stress to an already complicated life. They use your gift while ignoring your value.

God is not the author of confusion, so one way to discern if something is for you is to pay attention to the flow. That does not mean every assignment will be simple or effortless, but there will be a sense of alignment. The timing, the support, and the structure will bear witness that you are in the right lane. When everything around an opportunity feels forced, foggy, and frantic, it may be a sign to pause and ask, "Is this really mine to do?"

If you are feeling stretched thin, underappreciated, or pulled in too many directions, this might be a place where God is inviting you to re-evaluate how you see your worth. Not to run from responsibility, but to release what does not align. To believe that your time, your gifts, and your presence carry weight. To trust that you do not have to accept every request in order to honor God or prove your value to other people. Sometimes the most faithful answer you can give is no.

***Honor the work God gave you. Set boundaries that reflect your value, and let God lead your lane.***

# DAY 20

## Mile Marker 284.8: Seasons and Sacrifice

*"There is a time for everything, and a season for every activity under the heavens."*
ECCLESIASTES 3:1 (NIV)

The highway looked different this morning. I couldn't quite put my finger on it at first, but something had shifted. The trees along the route were changing. A few weeks ago, they were full and green, alive with summer's confidence. Now, patches of yellow and orange were creeping in, quiet signals that fall was coming.

I was thinking about sacrifice and in a season of pushing my dreams forward. Really focused. Really intentional. And with that focus came some difficult choices. I had to sacrifice things I normally would have done. Fishing trips I didn't take. Friends I hadn't seen in weeks. Time I used to spend scrolling or relaxing, but redirected toward building something that mattered.

That day, the fields on either side of the highway stretched out wide and empty. Harvest season was near. I thought about how farmers sacrifice too. They plant in spring, tend through summer, and wait. They do not get to enjoy the seed. They must trust the process and let time do its work. That is where I was, and where I am now. Planting. Tending. Trusting.

Here is what I have learned: whenever you are focused on a goal, there has to be a level of sacrifice. You either sacrifice relationships, money, habits that do not move you forward, or comfort, choosing the hard work of building over the ease of coasting.

I passed a sign for Sullivan, and my mind went to the three D's that try to creep in when you are locked in: doubt, discouragement, and distraction. Doubt whispers that maybe you are doing too much. Discouragement comes from people who do not mean harm but offer opinions based on where they sit, not where you are going. And distraction is the enemy on assignment, trying to pull you away from what God called you to do.

Sacrifice is the cost of progress. The trees do not resist the fall. They let go of what they carried all summer so they can prepare for what is next. And when spring comes, they will bloom again, stronger than before.

If you are in a season where you have had to pull back, cut off, or say no more than yes, do not feel guilty. You are not abandoning people. You are not being selfish. You are being obedient to the assignment in front of you.

The things that matter will be understood. And the things that do not, will fall away like leaves in October.

**Sacrifice isn't loss. It's the price of becoming who you're meant to be.**

# DAY 21

## Mile Marker 303: The Choice Is Yours

*"This day I call the heavens and the earth as witnesses against you that I have set before you life and death, blessings and curses. Now choose life, so that you and your children may live."*

DEUTERONOMY 30:19 (NIV)

The way we view life has a direct impact on how we navigate each day. Responsibilities, challenges, and uninvited situations can make the road ahead feel heavy before the day even begins. But amid the noise of life, there is one question that can change everything: *What do you choose to do with what you have been given?*

A popular gospel song by Donnie McClurkin asks, "What do you do when you've done all you can, and it seems like it's never enough?" The answer, "You just stand," has inspired countless people to persevere. But over time, I learned that standing was only the beginning. To truly grow, I had to take intentional steps forward, even when the road felt uncertain.

Over the years, friends and loved ones often asked how I stayed so positive through life's "lemons." Yes, I made lemonade (thank you, Beyoncé), but there was more to it than that. Life, in its fullness, offered both mountaintop moments and valleys of difficulty. It was like driving through a long, winding highway. Sometimes I was coasting with the windows down. Other times, I was gripping the wheel in the rain. But neither the joy nor the pain was permanent.

One of the most powerful tools we have for navigating the road ahead is optimism. Optimism does not ignore reality; it reframes it. It helps you see possibilities where others see roadblocks. It gives you the courage to keep going when the journey gets rough.

I remember one season when everything seemed to fall apart. Finances, relationships, family matters—each colliding at once. For a while, I felt lost. Then one day, I made a choice: instead of focusing on what I could not control, I would focus on how I responded. That decision shifted everything. The road did not instantly smooth out, but my outlook changed, and that changed the journey.

What we put into the world often circles back. If you release bitterness, you attract more of it. But when you choose joy, kindness, and gratitude, those same forces return to strengthen you. The road may not always lead where you expect, but how you travel it is always your choice.

So, on this day, although I dreaded waking up and getting on that highway, I knew, like the sun, life would eventually burn off the morning fog. Look at the miles behind you and the road ahead, and decide: *Will you let this moment define you, or will you define it?*

Because the truth is, the choice has always been yours.

**You can't always choose the road, but you can choose how you travel it.**

# DAY 22

## Mile Marker 302: Making Room

*"I press on toward the goal to win the prize for which God has called me heavenward in Christ Jesus."*

PHILIPPIANS 3:14 (NIV)

This morning, I left the house wearing a shirt I knew didn't fit right. It was a little too short, a little too tight, and honestly, I should have put it in the donation pile months ago. But I grabbed it anyway, put it on, and walked out the door. By the time I hit the on-ramp, I was already regretting it.

The seatbelt tugged at the fabric, making me shift every few minutes. I kept adjusting it, trying to find comfort, but nothing worked. As I drove, the discomfort grew beyond physical—it became symbolic.

As I got on the road, I thought about my closet—particularly the shirts I keep despite knowing they no longer serve me. I realized I hold on to things just because they've been there, not because they truly help me. Then the words dropped into my spirit again: What do you keep holding on to?

Near Mile Marker 302, I saw a truck carrying what appeared to be old furniture—worn-out couches, outdated dressers—things once valued but now discarded. It made me reflect on how we similarly hold on to things in life: relationships that drain us, habits that numb us, and routines that no longer match who we're becoming.

We keep them because they're familiar. Because letting go feels like loss. Because we convince ourselves that someday, somehow, they'll fit again. However, the longer you hold on to what doesn't fit, the less room you have for what will.

I thought about my job, friendships, goals, and the person I'm becoming. I realized that some attachments hinder my growth, and the elevation God has prepared for me. It's not that those things were bad or useless. They once served a purpose, like the shirt I outgrew. Forcing it now only makes me uncomfortable.

The same goes for everything else—the relationship where you're the only one investing, the mindset that keeps you playing small, the habit you know you should break but keep revisiting because it's easier than change.

Holding on to it doesn't honor what it was. It just blocks what's trying to come next.

Later that evening, when I got home, I made the decision that I would clean out my closet—not with regret, but with gratitude. Grateful for what those shirts represented in a season that's now behind me. And faithful for what's ahead.

Maybe you need to do the same—not with clothes, but with whatever you're holding on to that no longer serves you. When you release it, you create space. And in that space, something better will come.

**What you release makes room for what will elevate you.**

# DAY 23

## Mile Marker 294.2: The Season of Ideas

*"To everything there is a season, and a time to every purpose under the heaven."*
ECCLESIASTES 3:1 (KJV)

It's always somewhere between Johnson Creek and Lake Mills when my phone goes crazy. Another idea. Another concept. Another project that demanded my attention. I didn't answer it right away. I just let it sit there, knowing it would join the list of things swirling in my mind.

Lately, it felt like ideas wouldn't stop coming. I'd be sitting somewhere, minding my business, and suddenly a complete vision would drop into my spirit—a book, a message, a strategy—something that needed to be created, released, and shared with the world. And with every new idea came a question: Was I moving too fast?

The highway was quiet that morning. The sun was still climbing, painting the fields in soft gold. I thought about how often I'd doubted myself for producing too quickly—publishing books back-to-back, releasing content at a pace that felt almost reckless, wondering if people would think I was sacrificing quality for speed. But then I thought about my brother, a well-known artist who drops songs constantly. He doesn't wait for permission. He doesn't second-guess the flow. When creativity comes, he releases it. And people receive it because it's authentic.

I passed the Pine Cone restaurant and thought about seasons. Fall doesn't ask permission to arrive. Winter doesn't apologize for showing up on schedule. Spring doesn't hesitate to bloom. They come when they're supposed to, and everything in nature responds. That's what I'd been feeling—a season, a flow, a divine rhythm that I couldn't control and shouldn't resist.

When God gives you something, it's your responsibility to get it out into the world. Not next year. Not when it's convenient. Not when you've overthought it into perfection. Now. In the season He gives it to you. Because here's the thing: seasons don't wait. If you sit on what God gives you, your moment will pass.

Someone else will say what you were supposed to say. The door He opens will close. And you'll be left wondering why the momentum stopped.

I didn't have time to sit around and ponder. I didn't have time to worry about what people would think or whether they'd criticize the pace. The thing I was being inspired to do was for somebody on the other side who was waiting for it. So, I made my peace with the speed. I accepted that this season was about output, not hesitation. And I trusted that what God gave me in the flow was exactly what someone else needed in their famine.

The exit for Lake Mills came into view, and I exhaled. The ideas weren't a burden. They were a blessing. And my job wasn't to manage them. It was to release them.

If you're in a season where creativity is pouring out of you, don't slow down to please people. Don't dim your output because others aren't moving at your pace. Stay in your lane. Trust the flow. And get it out while you're in the season.

**What God gives you in your season is for someone else's survival.**

# DAY 24

## Mile Marker 265.2: Your Assignment

*"For we are God's handiwork, created in Christ Jesus to do good works, which God prepared in advance for us to do."*

EPHESIANS 2:10 (NIV)

The road was empty this morning—just me, the highway, and my thoughts. The kind of quiet that makes you reflective, whether you want to be or not. I had my music off, my phone silent, and nothing to distract me from the question that had been sitting heavily on my heart: What is my assignment?

I passed a field where the crops had already been harvested. The land looked bare, but not empty. It was resting, preparing for the next season, waiting for what would be planted next. And I thought about how we are all like that—planted here for a reason, assigned something specific that only we can do.

But how often do we actually live in that truth? We spend so much time comparing our lives to others, watching their highlight reels, measuring our progress against their pace, and wondering why their lane seems to move faster than ours. In all that comparison, we lose sight of the one thing that matters most: our assignment.

Keyimani couldn't be Joe. Joe couldn't be Keyimani. Keyimani couldn't be Abigail. And Abigail couldn't be you. Each one of us has a unique, divine purpose—a specific assignment connected to who we are, where we've been, and what we're called to do.

The sun broke through the clouds ahead, and the highway lit up in gold. I thought about the people I'd met, the lives I'd touched, the conversations I'd had whose impact I might never fully understand. I realized my assignment wasn't about being the loudest or the fastest or the most successful. It was about being obedient to what God called me to do.

Your assignment isn't someone else's. It's yours. When you spend your energy trying to walk in someone else's shadow, you're not walking in your assignment. You're walking in their echo.

I passed Mile Marker 265.2 and whispered a prayer—not for clarity, because I already knew what I was called to do, but for focus, for the discipline to stay in my lane and trust that my assignment is enough.

You don't need to be anyone else. You don't need to copy their strategy or mimic their style. You need to show up as yourself and do what God put you here to do.

When you stop comparing, you start creating. And when you start creating from your assignment, the world receives what only you can give.

***Your assignment is yours alone. Walk in it without apology.***

# DAY 25

## Mile Marker 275.6: What I Trust

*"Trust in the LORD with all your heart and lean not on your own understanding; in all your ways submit to him, and he will make your paths straight."*

PROVERBS 3:5-6 (NIV)

Can I be honest with you? Trusting a process is not the easiest thing to do. We often have dreams, aspirations, and goals that we want to accomplish in life but the journey to get them often feels long, dreadful, and tiring.

Many days on my drive back and forth between Milwaukee and Madison, my mind would hover around the fact that I often felt that I should be further along in life. I should've won the lottery, own a mansion, have a partner–kids even. Yet, my reality seems to provide me with a different outcome.

On this particular drive, I was cruising down the highway, mostly with my phone in my hand – one of the crazy ways that I pass time during the hour or so drive – and during that time I thought about life. My thoughts are usually deep in the middle of the trip, so this time I was around Mile Marker 275.6. I called myself talking to God and asking Him some really hard questions, questions that seemed to always hover around the word, "Why?" You know, we sometimes do that when we recognize that we want things to be different than they are. We're operating on our timing and not trusting God's. Isn't that ironic? We want what He has for us, but don't want to abide by the timeframe that He wants to give it to us. How ungrateful is that, or how spoiled are we as His children?

Nevertheless, during this moment of talking with God, I began to wonder why I wasn't experiencing the seasons that I felt I should be in. Then, He did something that I didn't necessarily expect. He told me. God said, "The reason why you're not experiencing what you desire is because you're not ready for it. You're leaning into your understanding where I have bigger plans for you."

Wow! How often do we seek and desire something but fail to know that even the grandest ideas and vision that we have for ourselves is nothing compared to what God has for us? How amazing is that?

After that conversation, I decided to shut up and trust the process and make sure that the things that I do now and in the future are aligned in His will for my life. We can dream dreams, have the biggest goals, but even in those moments, they are only glimpses into what God says that we can have. And the amazing part about it all is that it's created and designed specifically for us!

As you continue to move throughout your day, I want to encourage you to trust the process and allow God to organize all of the opportunities that will come your way. However, while you wait, ensure that you make this your prayer: Dear God, allow me to be ready to handle every blessing that you have in store for me. If I am ready for it then I will honor the gift that you place before me. Amen.

**God always knows what is best for us at the time when it will be best for us. Trust the process and his leading.**

# DAY 26

## Mile Marker 250.2: Facing Yourself

*"Search me, God, and know my heart; test me and know my anxious thoughts."*
PSALM 139:23 (NIV)

The highway was clear, but my mind wasn't. I had been wrestling with something for days. Not a person. Not a situation. Myself. The trees on either side of the road blurred past as I pressed the gas a little harder. I wasn't in a rush to get anywhere. I was trying to outrun a thought that wouldn't let me go. A dream I had that felt too big. A goal that seemed too bold. A version of myself I wanted to become but wasn't sure I could. And every time I got close to believing in it, another voice rose up. Not someone else's voice. Mine.

You're not ready for that. You don't have what it takes. Who do you think you are?

I passed Mile Marker 250.2, and the irony wasn't lost on me. I was moving forward on the highway, but in my head, I was standing still. Sabotaging myself with my own thoughts. Discrediting my potential before I even gave myself a chance to try.

Why do we do that?

The fields to my right were being prepared for planting. The soil had been turned over, dark and rich, waiting for seed. And I thought about how the farmer couldn't stop halfway. If they did, half the field would produce, and half wouldn't. The work would be wasted. The potential would be lost.

That's what I was doing. Sitting on potential. Holding a dream in my hand and refusing to plant it because I was afraid it wouldn't grow.

The most difficult thing I've had to do in my own life is face myself. Not in the mirror. Not in a literal sense. But in my thoughts. In the battle between what I believe I can do and what I'm afraid I can't.

I thought about the other side of risk. The phrase I'd used in my own reflections before. On the other side of risk is reward. But you have to face the fear first. You must confront the voice that says you're not enough and challenge it with the truth that God doesn't call the qualified. He qualifies the called.

I've been willing to do hard things. But willing doesn't always mean able. And able doesn't always mean I have the willpower to see it through. That's where the real fight is. Not in the doing. But in the deciding. In choosing to act even when my mind is throwing up every reason not to.

The truth is, the only thing that stops us from being, doing, or becoming is ourselves. Not other people. Not circumstances. Not lack of opportunity. Us. Our doubts. Our fears. Our refusal to believe that what God placed in us is enough.

I passed the exit for Johnson Creek and exhaled. I wasn't going to turn around. Not on the highway. Not in my head. I was going to keep moving forward, even if it felt uncomfortable. Even if the voice in my head tried to convince me to stop.

Because what God has for me is for me. And the only person who can keep me from it is the one staring back at me in the rearview mirror.

**The only thing stopping you from becoming is you.**

# DAY 27

## Mile Marker 258.4: What Sustains You

*"The LORD is my shepherd, I lack nothing. He makes me lie down in green pastures, he leads me beside quiet waters, he refreshes my soul."*

PSALM 23:1-3 (NIV)

The road was quiet this morning. Almost too quiet. I had my window cracked just enough to let the cool air in, and the only sound was the gentle hum of the engine beneath me. My mind, though, was loud. I was thinking about what sustains us. Not the surface-level stuff. Not the accolades or the applause or the notifications that make us feel seen for a moment. But the deep stuff. The foundation. The thing that keeps us going when everything else falls away.

I passed a farm where the barn looked old but sturdy. Weathered by years but still standing. It had survived storms I'd never known about. Winters that tried to break it. Seasons that tested its structure. And yet, it was still there.

I thought about my own work. The books I've written. The speaking engagements. The posts that get shared, liked, and commented on. All of it feels good. All of it matters. But what happens when the book sales slow down? When the speaking invitations stop coming? When the engagement fades and the noise quiets?

What sustains me then?

The answer came to me somewhere between exits. It's not the work. It's not the recognition. It's the values. The morals. The truth I stand on when everything else is shaken.

I've built my life on principles that don't change with the season. Integrity. Faith. Service. Compassion. Those things don't need an audience to matter. They don't need applause to be real. They sustain me when nothing else can.

As the highway curved gently to the left, I thought about social media. How we see people's highlight reels and assume their lives are easy. We see the glitz and the glamour and think they've figured it out. But behind the scenes, most of us are grinding. Struggling. Questioning. Working late nights and waking up early to build something that might not even be seen.

It's not as easy as it looks. It takes grit. It takes persistence. It takes a belief in something bigger than the immediate reward.

And when the world isn't receiving what I'm putting out, when the work feels invisible, when the results don't match the effort, the only thing that keeps me going is knowing I'm grounded in something that can't be shaken.

I passed Mile Marker 258.4 and whispered a prayer. Not for success. Not for recognition. But for endurance. For the strength to keep going when the applause fades. For the faith to believe that what I'm building matters, even when no one's watching.

Because the truth is, what sustains you in the valleys is the same thing that will carry you to the peaks. And if your foundation isn't built on something solid, the first storm will knock you down.

*What sustains you when everything else falls away is all that truly matters.*

# DAY 28

## Mile Marker 276.2: The Three D's

*"Stay alert! Watch out for your great enemy, the devil. He prowls around like a roaring lion, looking for someone to devour."*

1 PETER 5:8 (NLT)

Buzz. Buzz. There it was again, my phone lighting up while driving on the highway. It was a message from someone I hadn't heard from in a while. I glanced at it quickly as I pulled off the road to get gas, and my chest tightened. It wasn't malicious or even intentionally discouraging, but the words carried weight.

"Are you sure about that? Have you thought about what could go wrong?"

I put the phone down, got into my car, and pulled away from the gas pump on the highway. The road ahead was clear, but my mind wasn't. That message sat heavy in my spirit, and I realized something I'd felt before but never named.

When you're working on something that matters, when you have a dream you're chasing, the three D's will always show up: **doubt, discouragement, and distraction**.

While driving, I notice that the fields off the side of the highway were wide and open. Harvest was over, and the land looked bare. I thought about farmers and how they plant in faith, knowing there's no guarantee. They can't control the weather. They can't force the crops to grow. But they plant anyway, trusting the process.

That's where I was. Planting. Trusting. Moving forward. And yet, the three D's kept showing up.

Doubt came first. It sounded like my own voice, questioning whether I had what it took. Whether the work I was doing was good enough. Whether anyone would even care.

Discouragement came second. Sometimes from people who meant well but couldn't see what I was building. They'd offer opinions based on where they were sitting, not where I was going. And even though they didn't mean harm, their words planted seeds of hesitation.

Distraction came last. The enemy on assignment, trying to pull my focus away from what God called me to do. A notification here. An opportunity there. Something shiny and appealing that looked good but wasn't aligned with my purpose.

Leaving the gas station, there is a stop sign that says, "WHOA" instead of "STOP." That sign always made me smile. And at that moment, I thought about how that word applied here. Whoa. Slow down. Pay attention. Recognize what's happening before you get derailed.

The three D's are real, but they only have power if you give them attention. Doubt only wins if you stop moving. Discouragement only sticks if you let it rewrite your vision. Distraction only works if you take your eyes off the goal.

So, when they show up, and they will, you must make a choice. Will you let them define your journey, or will you keep driving? I now realize the three D's were passengers I didn't invite, but I refuse to let them steer, and you shouldn't either.

***Doubt, discouragement, and distraction will come. Don't let them drive.***

# DAY 29

## Mile Marker 262.6: The Cost of Haste

*"The plans of the diligent lead to profit as surely as haste leads to poverty."*
PROVERBS 21:5 (NIV)

Here we go again, another one of those mornings that demanded my patience. I was off from work but still had to make my usual early drive to Madison for a 6:00 a.m. flight. I liked early flights, yet I often tested my luck by packing too late, forgetting something at home, or arriving at the airport within an hour of departure without counting the time it takes to park and get through security. TSA PreCheck usually gave me an advantage when I traveled, but that day was different.

I decided to be more mindful and planned to leave by 4:15 a.m. It was an hour to Madison, and because it was a smaller airport, I assumed it would be easy to get to my gate. There was one thing I miscalculated: I had to check a bag.

I was flying to San Francisco to take my mom on a birthday trip, a destination I hoped she would enjoy, and I was also going early to help her get ready.

Out of the house I went, in my car, passing mile markers and reflecting. Then it hit me. Shoot, I must check this bag. That quiet drive turned into a speedway. Seventy, then eighty, then ninety miles per hour became my top speed. I was determined to reach the airport in time to get that bag on the plane.

After about forty-five minutes of speeding, I made it. I found a parking spot and dashed to the counter. It was thirty minutes before departure. The clerk asked my destination. I told her. She responded, "It's too late to get your bags on the plane." The gate had closed.

I stood there in shock and with understanding, because sometimes what we experience comes from our own decisions. I was up early enough, but I played with time, and the result was missing my flight. I had to wait four hours for the next one, and I had to accept it.

You may not be missing a flight today, but you might be delaying a goal because you feel you do not have all the tools yet. Maybe it is a project you keep putting off because starting feels heavy. Delays cause consequences. No matter what you do, there is always one. The good news is you can choose a better consequence by choosing diligence over hurry.

Choose wisdom today. Plan ahead. Count back from your deadline and give yourself margin. Pack the night before, set the alarm fifteen minutes earlier than you think you need, and leave when you said you would. Tackle the goal in front of you with steady steps, and let diligence do its work.

As you think about the future, consider reflecting on where you are cutting it close, and calling it faith. I believe discovering that will help unlock your ability to be patient and not miss the things that matter during your journey.

*Patience with planning protects your purpose.*

# DAY 30

## Mile Marker 272.8: Deleting the Dead Weight

*"Make every effort to live in peace with everyone and to be holy; without holiness no one will see the Lord."*

HEBREWS 12:14 (NIV)

Traffic was unusually heavy this morning. I sat in a line of brake lights, inching forward, watching the clock on my dashboard tick away minutes I didn't have. I pulled out my phone and started scrolling through Facebook to pass the time.

That's when I saw it. Another friend request notification. But when I tried to accept it, I got a message: "You've reached the maximum number of friends."

Five thousand. I'd hit the limit.

I sat there staring at the screen, and something stirred in me. There were people waiting to connect with me, but I had no room. My list was full. Full of profiles that weren't even active anymore. Full of people with multiple accounts taking up space. Full of connections that no longer served a purpose.

Traffic started moving again, and I put the phone down. But the thought stayed with me. I passed Pewaukee, with the lake shimmering in the morning light. I thought about how still the water looked on the surface, but underneath, there was always movement. Things growing. Things dying. Things being filtered out so the ecosystem could stay healthy.

That's what I needed to do. Filter. Delete. Make room.

When I got home that night, I did it. I went through my friends list, name by name, and started deleting. Inactive profiles. Duplicate accounts. People I didn't even remember adding. It took hours. It was tedious. But with every deletion, I felt lighter.

Here's a shocking truth: there are people occupying space in your life who no longer serve a purpose. Not because they're bad people or don't care. But because their season with you has ended.

I thought about the people who were waiting to connect with me. The ones who might have a blessing attached to my destiny. The ones who might have the resources to catapult my career. The ones who might have the encouragement to shift my mindset. But they couldn't get in because I was holding onto people who were no longer present.

God connects us to people for a lifetime, but He also connects us to people for a season. And it's important to know the difference.

I passed Mile Marker 272.8 the next morning, and my phone felt different. Lighter. Like I'd made space for something new. And I realized that sometimes, the breakthrough you're waiting for is blocked by the dead weight you're refusing to release.

Maybe it's not a Facebook list for you. Maybe it's a relationship that's run its course. A friendship that's become one-sided. A commitment that no longer aligns with where you're going. Whatever it is, if it's taking up space and not adding value, it's time to let it go. Because the people who are supposed to connect with you can't get in if there's no room.

***Making space for new connections requires releasing old ones.***

# DAY 31

## Mile Marker 263.2: Being a Student

*"Let the wise listen and add to their learning, and let the discerning get guidance."*
PROVERBS 1:5 (NIV)

I was driving to Madison for a meeting, and my mind was already racing ahead. I was thinking about what I wanted to say, how I wanted to present my ideas, and what impression I wanted to leave. I wanted to be seen, heard, and valued.

But somewhere near Oconomowoc, a different thought dropped in: When was the last time you were a student?

Not in the literal sense. I wasn't talking about enrolling in a class or earning another degree. I was talking about posture—the willingness to sit at the feet of wisdom and learn from the people around me.

That morning, the highway was open, and I thought about how many times I had been in conversations where I was so focused on what I was going to say next that I missed what was being said to me. How many times had I walked into a room thinking I had all the answers, only to realize later that I had missed the lesson?

I passed the hospital on my right and thought about doctors. They spend years in school, then years in residency, learning from those who have done it before them. And even after they become experts, they keep learning. Still studying. Still humbling themselves to new information.

Why don't we do that in life with our situations? Sometimes we face the same challenges again and again, patterns we cannot seem to break. And I realized something: maybe we were repeating them because we didn't learn the lesson the first time.

Maybe we keep living paycheck to paycheck because we haven't learned to manage our money. Maybe we keep ending up in the same toxic relationships because we haven't done the inner work to recognize the red flags. Or, like me, maybe we keep hitting a toe on the same corner of the dresser because we refuse to get a nightlight.

In this season, winter was coming, and the trees along the highway were bare, stripped down to their core. They weren't resisting it. They were preparing for it, resting, getting ready for the next season of growth.

That's what being a student looks like. It is humbling yourself enough to admit you don't know everything. It is leaning into conversations with people who have wisdom you don't. It is recognizing that the situation you are in might be a test you need to pass before you can move forward.

Mile Marker 263.2 allowed me to make a commitment. The next time I walked into a room, I wasn't going to focus on being the smartest person there. I was going to focus on being the most willing to learn.

Life is constantly teaching. The moment you think you have learned it all is the moment you stop growing. So, here is my question for you: How often are you being a student? Are you humble enough to listen? Willing enough to learn? Open enough to admit when you don't have the answers? The situation you are facing might be a lesson you haven't passed yet.

***The moment you stop learning is the moment you stop growing.***

# DAY 32

## Mile Marker 304.6: And Then?

*"Therefore encourage one another and build each other up, just as in fact you are doing."*
1 THESSALONIANS 5:11 (NIV)

On my way home from work, I started thinking about a scene from one of my favorite movies, Dude, Where's My Car? There's this moment where two guys are at a drive-through, ordering food, and the person taking their order keeps saying, "And then? And then? And then?" It was funny in the movie. As the miles passed, I realized it's not so funny in leadership.

The road was open, and the sun set behind me, casting long shadows across the highway. I thought about the people I had led, the teams I had managed, and the individuals who looked to me for direction, inspiration, and support. I asked myself, What was my "and then"? As leaders, people come to us with expectations. They're looking for us to show up. To inspire, guide, and see them. And too often, we stop at the bare minimum. We give the task. We provide direction. Then we move on. We forget to ask, And then what do you need from me?

I passed a semi-truck hauling grain, and I thought about harvest. A farmer doesn't just plant the seed and walk away. They tend to the soil. They water. They protect the crop from pests. They monitor growth. They invest in the process all the way through to harvest.

That's what leadership should look like. It's not just about assigning tasks or setting expectations. It's about checking in. Following up. Asking what else your people need to succeed.

Because if you're not asking, "And then," you're leaving them incomplete. I thought about the times I'd felt unsupported as an employee. The moments when I was given a project but not the resources. The times I was expected to perform but not equipped to succeed. And I realized that the leaders who impacted me most were the ones who didn't just assign work. They asked what else I needed.

And then? What support can I provide?

And then? What obstacles are in your way?

And then? How can I help you win?

That's the difference between managing and leading. Management gives tasks. Leadership gives support.

The sky was turning shades of pink and orange now, and the highway felt peaceful. I thought about the people I'm responsible for. The ones who are counting on me to not just show up, but to show up fully.

And I made a commitment. I wasn't going to stop at the assignment. I was going to ask the follow-up question. I was going to check in. I was going to make sure they had everything they needed to succeed.

Because leadership isn't just about what you give. It's about what you give after that.

*Great leaders don't stop at the task.*
*They ask, "And then what do you need?"*

# DAY 33

## Mile Marker 296.4: God's Timing, Not Mine

*"For everything there is a season, and a time for every matter under heaven."*
ECCLESIASTES 3:1 (ESV)

While driving to work one morning, my mind was spinning. I had been working on two books at the same time: *Oakland Hills, Milwaukee Rivers,* and *Unshaken Leadership*. Both were important to me and carried messages I believed in. But I was frustrated because the response to *Unshaken Leadership* wasn't what I expected when trying to push it forward.

I wanted both to succeed. I wanted both to be seen. But somewhere between Sullivan and Lake Mills, God checked me.

Not audibly, but clear enough that I had to pull my focus back to the road and really listen.

And God whispered to me and said, "I gave you the inspiration to write both books. But I didn't tell you to release them at the same time." I gripped the steering wheel a little tighter because He was right.

I had rushed. I had gotten excited about the second book and started promoting it before the first one had finished its work. I had divided my attention, split my energy, and diluted the message God gave me to share.

*Oakland Hills, Milwaukee Rivers* was a global message. A story that needed time to breathe. Time to reach the people it was meant to reach. And instead of trusting the process, I had moved on to the next thing.

I thought about farmers again. How they don't plant two crops in the same field at the same time. They focus on one harvest. They give it everything. And when that season is complete, they prepare for the next. That's what I needed to do.

The sun started to break through the clouds, and the frost on the fields glistened like diamonds. I thought about the impact *Oakland Hills* was supposed to have. The lives it was meant to touch. The conversations it was meant to start.

And I realized that if I wanted to see the fullness of what God intended, I had to give it my full attention. I had to get back to the assignment He gave me first.

Not because the second book didn't matter. But because everything has its time. And when you move ahead of God's timing, you miss the fullness of what He's trying to do.

I passed Mile Marker 296.4 and decided, *Unshaken Leadership* was going on the back burner. My focus was going back to *Oakland Hills*. I was going to trust the process. Trust the timing. Trust that God knew what He was doing when He gave me the first assignment.

Because promotion without preparation is pressure. And I didn't want to carry the weight of trying to do two things when God only asked me to do one. When I obeyed, He showed me exactly why the conversation was necessary. Podcasts, book clubs, and radio interviews all came after.

So, here's my encouragement to you: don't rush the process. Don't move ahead of God's timing just because you're excited about what's next. Finish what He gave you first. Give it your full attention. And trust that when the season is right, He'll release the next thing.

**God's timing is better than your hustle.**

# DAY 34

## Mile Marker 289.8: You Belong Here

*"For we are God's handiwork, created in Christ Jesus to do good works, which God prepared in advance for us to do."*

EPHESIANS 2:10 (NIV)

Isn't it strange how often we apologize for who we are? We tone ourselves down, we shrink in certain spaces, and we question if we even belong. But the truth is, we were all created for a reason. Each of us has a unique contribution that no one else can bring.

This hit me while on a trip in Washington, DC. I was sitting in a room full of brilliant, educated leaders—people shaping the future of higher education. We were there to reflect on what it might mean to step into the role of a college or university president one day.

The perspectives were diverse. The experiences were different. Then one of the presenters said something that stuck with me: "Every single one of you has what it takes to be a president. Otherwise, you wouldn't be in this room."

That moment made me pause. How many times do we discount ourselves? How often do we forget that the very fact we are in the room means we already bring value? That experience validated something in me: I am more than enough. And so are you.

Your past—your ups, your downs, your lessons, your mistakes—is not a disqualifier. It is shaping the person your future will need. So, stop apologizing for who you are. Stop shrinking. Stop questioning whether you are worthy. You already have everything you need for what is ahead.

Often in life we forget that God is intentional and if He is that it also means that He knew exactly what he was doing by ensuring that you were a staple in the world that we now dwell in.

As you navigate life and step into spaces, grasp the fact that your existence brings uniqueness and it cannot be duplicated or imitated no matter how much someone else tries.

***Your presence is proof that you belong.***
***Your today is preparing you for tomorrow.***

# DAY 35

## Mile Marker 293.2: Stop Seeking Validation

*"Am I now trying to win the approval of human beings, or of God? Or am I trying to please people? If I were still trying to please people, I would not be a servant of Christ."*

GALATIANS 1:10 (NIV)

While sitting at a red light, I glanced over and saw someone in the car next to me. They were on their phone, scrolling, smiling at something on the screen. For a split second, I wondered what they were looking at. What post had their attention? What validation they were getting from whatever they saw.

The light turned green, and I pulled forward. But the thought stayed with me.

We spend so much time seeking approval. Waiting for someone to tell us we're good enough, smart enough, talented enough, worthy enough. We post, we share, we create, and then we sit back and wait for the likes, the comments, the affirmation that what we did mattered. What if we stopped giving other people the power to validate who we are?

The highway opened ahead of me, wide and clear. I thought about a friend I used to know, an artist who constantly changed her style to please critics. She painted what she thought people wanted to see, not what was in her heart. The more she did that, the less her work felt like hers.

One day, she decided to paint something just for herself. No audience in mind. No approval she was chasing. Just her, the canvas, and the vision in her head.

That painting became her masterpiece. Not because it was technically perfect, but because it was authentically hers. In that authenticity, she found something she had been searching for all along: validation from within.

I passed a church on the right and thought about how often we look outside ourselves for the confirmation that should come from inside. We let other people's opinions shape our decisions. We let their expectations define our worth. We let their voices drown out the one that matters most, our own.

Here's the truth: you're already worthy. You don't need someone else to tell you that. Validation is seeking approval from others to feel valuable. You were born valuable. God didn't make a mistake when He made you. He didn't create you to spend your life waiting for someone else to say you're enough. You are enough. Right now. As you are.

I passed Mile Marker 293.2 and made a decision. I wasn't going to give anyone else the power to validate my work, my worth, or my calling. I was going to trust the voice inside me. The one who knows what I'm capable of. The one that God speaks through.

The outside voices don't matter. They change with the wind. They praise you one day and criticize you the next. The voice inside is the one you can trust.

So, stop seeking validation from people who don't have the authority to define you. Embrace who you are. Trust your instincts. Let that inner voice be the loudest in your life.

*Your worth isn't determined by someone else's opinion.*

# DAY 36

## Mile Marker 303.6: What You're Not Changing

*"Choose my instruction instead of silver, knowledge rather than choice gold."*
PROVERBS 8:10 (NIV)

The highway was packed this morning. I sat in bumper-to-bumper traffic, watching the same brake lights flash on and off in front of me. It was frustrating. I had somewhere to be, and the world wasn't cooperating.

Then I thought about a quote I heard recently: "Whatever you're not changing, you're choosing." It hit me harder than it should have. I thought about a friend who's been going through a rough patch. He complains about his situation constantly—his job, his relationships, his finances. Every conversation is the same. The same problems. The same frustrations. The same complaints. But nothing changes. Not because he can't change it, but because he won't.

Traffic started moving again, and I pressed the gas. I thought about how often we do this. We complain about things we have the power to fix. We stay in situations that drain us. We tolerate behaviors we know are wrong. We accept less than we deserve. Then we wonder why nothing gets better. The truth is, if you're not doing anything to change it, you're choosing it.

That job you hate? You're choosing to stay. That relationship that's one-sided? You're choosing to accept it. That habit that's holding you back? You're choosing to keep it.

I passed the Culver's in Lake Mills and thought about comfort. How we cling to what's familiar even when it's hurting us. Change is uncomfortable. It requires risk. It demands action. And sometimes it feels easier to complain than to do the work.

Here's what I've learned: complaining without action is just noise.

If you're going to bring up a problem, be willing to contribute to the solution. If you're going to point out what's wrong, be ready to do something about it. Otherwise, you're not being honest about wanting change—you're just venting.

And venting without action doesn't move you forward. It keeps you stuck.

I thought about the areas in my own life where I had been choosing discomfort over change: the habits I kept saying I'd break but never did, the relationships that needed boundaries I never set, and the situations I tolerated because confronting them felt harder than enduring them.

And I made a decision. I wasn't going to complain anymore about things I had the power to change. I was going to take action. Set boundaries. Make hard decisions. And trust that the discomfort of change was better than the pain of staying the same.

Because whatever you're not changing, you're choosing. And if you don't like what you're experiencing, it's time to make a different choice.

***If you're not changing it, you're choosing it.***

# DAY 37

## Mile Marker 256.2: Celebrate Their Season

*"Love one another with brotherly affection. Outdo one another in showing honor."*
ROMANS 12:10 (ESV)

Today started like one of those "get your butt out of the bed and get moving" mornings. I dragged myself up, did what I needed to do to get ready for work, and started looking for something to wear, even though I knew I should have picked my clothes out the night before. It was a crisp fall day, the kind where the sky was starting to clear, the sun was pushing its way up, and the light was just bright enough to make you squint and wish you had sunglasses in the car. Everything seemed to be moving smoothly as I pulled out from my apartment and headed toward the highway. There were a couple of little detours and a car in front of me with a driver who actually wanted to follow the speed limit while everyone else was trying to rush to wherever they needed to be.

I passed the Denny's on North Avenue and merged onto the highway like I normally would. As I settled into the drive, a song by Darrel Petties and Take 2 started playing in my mind. The song is called "Word," and some of the lyrics say, "Lord, I believe every word You said. I'm still alive because of what You said. Times get hard like they are right now, I'm going to hold on to Your Word." I had not even played the song yet that morning. It was just resting in my spirit. Those words reminded me how often I have had to lean on what God has spoken when life feels heavy and uncertain.

Somewhere in the flow of traffic, I did what I sometimes do. I picked up my phone and quickly checked a few things to get my mind ready for the day. Instead of opening Facebook, I opened LinkedIn. The first post I saw was a familiar one: "I'm happy to share that I've transitioned into a new position…" It was the kind of update you often see on LinkedIn. People getting promoted. People stepping into new roles. People retiring. People celebrating the next season of their professional lives.

As I read that post, it made me pause. I started thinking about a conversation I had with myself not long ago. I told myself that once the renovation project at work was finished, I would start intentionally looking at new opportunities. I wanted to see how I could use my gifts to help move the needle in higher education in new ways. That desire is still there, but the truth is, I have not taken any real steps yet. Even with that reality sitting with me, my first response to that post was simple. I clicked the celebration emoji with the clapping hands and congratulated the person who had just stepped into their new position.

I did that because I believe it is part of our responsibility to celebrate others while they are in their season. One day, that moment will come back around to us too. That LinkedIn post took my mind back to something I wrote during our spring graduation. I talked about how we need to learn how to celebrate each other more. I remembered sitting in the audience, cheering for students whose names I did not even know. I was not the one on the stage, but I celebrated as if I was. There was something powerful about realizing that my joy from the seats could still add encouragement to someone standing under the lights.

My thoughts then went to all the books I have bought from other authors over the years. As a self-publishing author, I know what it means when someone chooses to invest in your work. While I am recording this reflection, I can look over and see a book titled *We Wish We Had Known: Everyday Tips for Consultants to Grow Your Business* by the Madison Area Business Consultants. I bought it because someone I know is an author in that book. It is more than pages and strategies. It is a small act of support that says, "I see you. I value what you created. Your work matters."

That is really what my mind was wrestling with on the drive that morning. How do we show up for each other in real, simple ways? How do we support people who are doing work similar to ours without seeing them as competition? How do we choose community, collaboration, and celebration instead of comparison? Sometimes all it takes is a small gesture, a comment, a purchase, a text, or a prayer. Those simple acts might only take us a few seconds, but for the person on the other end, that moment can stay with them for a lifetime.

Here is what I know: Celebration is a form of love. There is room for all of us. When we honor what God is doing in someone else, we make space in our own hearts to trust what God is doing in us. So, today do something simple and intentional for someone else to help them see you and not competition.

> ***Let your encouragement be a reminder that you trust***
> ***God with your own journey too.***

# DAY 38

## Mile Marker 292.4: The Weight of No

*"If you tell me no, it just means I'm talking to the wrong person."*
MILEY CYRUS

Silence filled the car as I stared at an email I didn't want to read. I already knew what it said before I opened it. Another rejection. Another "Thank you for your interest, but we've decided to move in a different direction." I put the phone down and started driving.

The highway was quiet, and the sky was overcast. Everything felt heavy. I thought about all the applications I had submitted. All the time I spent writing cover letters, uploading documents, and gathering references. All the hope I carried that maybe, just maybe, this one would be different.

But it wasn't.

I passed Nagawicka Lake off I-94, and it looked gray and still. I thought about how many times I had heard "no" in the past few months. From institutions. From organizations. From opportunities I believed were aligned with my calling.

Each "no" felt like a weight. A rejection. A statement that I wasn't good enough.

Then as I continued driving a different thought dropped in. A quote I had heard before but never really held onto: "If you tell me no, it just means I'm talking to the wrong person."

I let that sit for a minute.

What if the "no" wasn't about me? What if it wasn't a reflection of my worth or my capability? What if it was redirection?

I thought about God's timing. How He closes doors we want to walk through because He knows what's on the other side. How He protects us from situations that look good but would ultimately hurt us. How He redirects us toward something better, even when we can't see it yet.

The truth is, I am not supposed to be in every room I apply to. Some doors aren't meant for me. Not because I'm not qualified, but because that's not where God is leading me.

And the "no" I'm hearing isn't rejection. It's protection.

I reflected on how many times "no" saved me from something I would have regretted later. Jobs I didn't get that I'm now grateful I didn't take. Relationships that didn't work out that I'm thankful ended when they did. Opportunities that closed because something better was waiting.

The "no" wasn't the end. It was the redirection.

I passed Mile Marker 292.4 and exhaled. I wasn't going to let rejection break me. I was going to let it protect me. Because one day, I'll look back and realize that every "no" was leading me toward the "yes" I was meant to receive.

So, if you're facing rejection right now, don't let it define you. Let it redirect you. Trust that the door closing isn't punishment. It's protection. And the "yes" you're waiting for is still coming.

***Rejection isn't failure. It's redirection toward what's meant for you.***

# DAY 39

## Mile Marker 288.4: The Relationship That Matters

*"The reputation of how someone feels lasts longer than what you make them do."*

PERSONAL REFLECTION

I was driving home from work on a Friday afternoon when my phone rang. It was one of my best friends. I let it go to voicemail, not because I didn't want to talk, but because I was tired—drained from the week. I was focused on getting home and collapsing.

But the voicemail she left sat heavy in my spirit. "I miss you. I feel like we never talk anymore. I wish we spent more time together. I wish I was more of a priority in your life."

I pulled into a gas station near Lake Mills and sat there with the engine running. The words stung because they were true.

I had been busy. Building. Creating. Working. Chasing goals that mattered to me. But in all of that, I had let something else slip—the relationships that grounded me, the people who knew me before the books, before the platform, before any of this.

The sun was setting, and the sky was turning shades of orange and pink. I thought about all I had accomplished in the past few months. The milestones. The launches. The wins. And I realized none of it felt as good as it should have because the people I wanted to celebrate with weren't there.

Not because they didn't care, but because I hadn't made space for them.

I thought about a quote I wrote in my leadership book: The reputation of how someone feels lasts longer than what you make them do. People don't remember your résumé. They remember how you made them feel. And right now, the people closest to me were feeling forgotten.

I pulled back onto the highway and headed home. The road was almost empty, and the quiet gave me space to think. I thought about my calendar, my priorities, and the things I said mattered but didn't show up in how I spent my time. Work mattered. Building mattered. But relationships mattered more.

Here's the truth: you can build an empire and still be lonely. You can achieve every goal and still feel empty. You can be successful in every metric and still miss the point. The point is people. Connection. The moments that never make the highlight reel but fill your heart in ways nothing else can.

I passed Mile Marker 288.4, almost home, and made a decision. I was going to call her back. Not tomorrow. Not when I had time. Tonight. And I was going to do more than talk. I was going to show up, make plans, and be present.

Because the credentials I earn will fade. The accolades will be forgotten. But the way I made people feel will last.

So, here's my encouragement to you: if there are people in your life who matter, show them. Don't wait until you have time—make time. Don't wait until it's convenient—make it a priority. Because relationships mean something, and it's up to you to hold your end of the bar.

**What people remember most is how you made them feel.**

# DAY 40

## Mile Marker 280.6: Built Over Time

*"Do not despise these small beginnings, for the Lord rejoices to see the work begin."*
ZECHARIAH 4:10 (NLT)

There is a house on my way to Madison that has spoken me for a long time. It sits off the road near mile marker 280.6, on its own little plot of land, clean and contemporary. One morning I saw the owner pull into the driveway in a nice truck, and it all looked picture perfect. The kind of scene where you could easily say, "They made it."

But that is not what I see when I drive by now. When I look at that house, I remember when there was nothing there. Just land. Every trip back and forth to work, I watched that place change a little at a time. First, they tilled the ground. Then I saw concrete poured for the foundation. After that, wood went up for the frame. One day, the roof was on. Another day, the shingles were laid. Windows went in. Siding wrapped around the outside. Landscaping started to shape the yard. Over time, what used to be an empty field slowly became the house I see today.

Now it is fully complete and beautiful. If you drove past it for the first time today, you might think it was always that way. I know better. I watched the process. I watched it come together mile after mile, morning after morning. And somewhere in that story, there was also a family or an owner dreaming and planning long before any of us saw the first truck on the land.

I imagine them sitting at a table with a builder or architect, talking through every detail. What they wanted the front to look like. How many bedrooms. What kind of kitchen. Where the windows would be. How they wanted to feel when they pulled into that driveway at the end of a long day. Before there was ever a house to admire, there was a vision.

Then came the part nobody posts on social media. The waiting. The delays. The changes. Maybe they chose a certain finish and later learned it would cost more than they expected. Maybe material prices went up due to tariffs. Maybe the timeline shifted. Maybe something broke and had to be redone. There were probably days when it looked like nothing was happening at all, even though work was moving behind the scenes. It was still part of the build.

That house made me think about life. All of us have something we see in our minds. A future version of ourselves. A dream. A calling. A "one day" picture we carry in our hearts. Maybe it is a different role, a new city, a healthier lifestyle, a business, a book, or simply more peace. Sometimes we see someone else living in what looks like their finished house and something in us whispers, I wish I were there.

What we do not always see is their foundation season. The nights they questioned themselves. The mornings they started again. The sacrifices they made in private. The conversations where they had to pivot because the cost changed. The prayers they prayed when nothing seemed to be moving. Just like that house, their life was built piece by piece.

The same is true for us. Our lives are being built in stages. We want the finished picture, but God often walks us through the slow, steady work of construction. Pouring the concrete. Standing up the frame. Putting shingles on the roof, installing locks, or painting walls. None of these things look flashy, but they are all part of the structure.

Where we get discouraged is when we stare at our dirt and beams and compare it to someone else's finished front porch. We start to believe we are behind, or that nothing is happening for us. But if we could step back, we might realize God has us in the middle of our build, not at the end of our story.

You may be in a season where you feel like things should be further along. You might look at your life and only see pieces. I get that. I have been there. But from one traveler to another, I want to remind you that the story is still being built. Your foundation matters. Your framing matters. Your small steps matter.

One day, you will look back and realize you did not just arrive at a finished house. You watched it come together, slowly and faithfully, along the miles. And you will see that God was with you in every stage of the construction.

***Our destiny deserves to be built with quality and intention; but we must be willing to trust the process.***

# DAY 41

## Mile Marker 290.8: Stop Complaining

*"Do everything without grumbling or arguing."*
PHILIPPIANS 2:14 (NIV)

Stuck in traffic and the person in the car next to me looked miserable. On my daily commutes I often noticed things: people on their phones, women fixing their make-up, and others in deep conversation – sometimes with themselves or someone else. It was always so intriguing. On this day it was frustrating. I could see them through the window, shaking their head, talking to themselves, clearly frustrated about the delay. And I thought, I wonder if they complain about this every single day.

After about 10 minutes, traffic started moving again, and I settled back into my lane. But the thought stayed with me. Some people complain about everything. The job. The weather. The traffic. The people around them. Always something. Always negative. Always acting like the sky is falling.

But here's the thing: they never do anything about it. They wake up every day and repeat the same cycle. Same complaints. Same frustrations. Same refusal to change anything. And it's exhausting just being around them.

I passed a church on the right and thought about a quote I heard recently: Whatever you're not changing, you're choosing. If you're going to complain about something, do something about it. Otherwise, you're not being honest. You're not looking for a solution. You're just venting. And venting without action is just noise.

The highway opened ahead, and I thought about the people I know who complain constantly but never take responsibility. They want things to be different, but they are not willing to do the work to make it different. That job you hate? Find a new one. That relationship that drains you? Set boundaries or leave. That situation that is making you miserable? Change it. Because if you're not contributing to the solution, you're contributing to the problem.

I thought about my own life, the things I used to complain about until I realized I had the power to change them. The moment I stopped complaining and started acting, everything shifted. Complaining keeps you stuck. Action moves you forward.

I passed Mile Marker 290.8 and made a commitment. I wasn't going to be someone who complains without taking action. I wasn't going to waste energy on problems I wasn't willing to solve. Here's the truth: life will give you plenty of reasons to complain. But complaining doesn't change anything. Action does.

So, if there's something in your life that's bothering you, stop talking about it and do something about it. Set the boundary. Have the conversation. Make the change. Because whatever you're not changing, you're choosing. And if you don't like it, it's time to choose differently.

*__Complaining without action is just noise. Change requires movement.__*

# DAY 42

## Mile Marker 259.6: Out of Your Head

*"Do not be anxious about anything, but in every situation, by prayer and petition, with thanksgiving, present your requests to God."*

PHILIPPIANS 4:6 (NIV)

I was driving in silence this morning. No music. No podcast. Just me and my thoughts. And honestly, that's where I spend most of my time. In my head I think about everything—the work I'm doing, the goals I'm chasing, the decisions I've made, the ones I should have made differently. I replay conversations. I question choices. I wonder if I'm on the right path or if I've somehow missed a turn.

The highway was empty, and the morning light was soft. I passed a field being prepared for planting, and I thought about growth. How it happens slowly. How you can't see it day by day, but over time, something changes.

Then I thought about déjà vu.

I had one of those moments recently. I was walking out of my apartment, heading to the post office, and suddenly it hit me. I had been here before. Not physically, but in the feeling. The moment. The energy. Like I had lived this exact experience in another time.

They say déjà vu is a sign that you are on the right path, that you're exactly where you're supposed to be. And for someone like me, who spends way too much time questioning everything, that was a relief.

I passed a sign for Sullivan and thought about all the times I've second-guessed myself. Wondering if I made the right decision. If I'm doing enough. If I'm in the right place. If the work I'm putting in will actually lead somewhere.

Here's what I'm learning: not every thought deserves my attention.

Sometimes being in your head is helpful. It's reflective. It's where creativity happens. Other times, it's just noise. It's doubt disguised as wisdom. It's fear pretending to be discernment. And the more I feed those thoughts, the more they control me.

I thought about all the energy I've wasted questioning decisions I already made. Worrying about outcomes I can't control. Stressing over things that haven't even happened yet. And I realized something: I need to get out of my head and into my life.

Life is happening now. Not in the future I'm planning for. Not in the past I'm replaying. Now. And if I'm not present for it, I'm missing it.

I passed Mile Marker 259.6 and took a deep breath. I decided to trust the process. To trust that every decision I've made has led me to where I am. To stop second-guessing and start living.

You are good enough. What you're doing is good enough. You're going to see the results of your work. But not if you stay stuck in your head, paralyzed by doubt.

Here's my encouragement to you: get out of your head. Stop overanalyzing. Stop questioning every move. Trust that you're on the right path, and keep moving forward

***Being in your head too long will keep you from living your life.***

# DAY 43

## Mile Marker 282.8: Trust the Process

*"For I know the plans I have for you, declares the LORD, plans to prosper you and not to harm you, plans to give you hope and a future."*

JEREMIAH 29:11 (NIV)

My mind was heavy driving to work today. I had been working on launching a new website, thinking about my book, and considering the impact I wanted to make. Somewhere in all of that, doubt crept in. Was I doing enough? Was I moving fast enough? Was any of this going to work?

The questions piled on top of each other until I felt the weight of them pressing on my chest. The road ahead was clear, but I wasn't. I was stuck in my own uncertainty, questioning everything I had been building. I passed a construction site where a new building was going up. The foundation had been poured weeks ago, but now the walls were starting to rise. Slowly. One beam at a time. It didn't look impressive yet, but it was progress. And I thought about how building anything worthwhile takes time.

We live in a world that celebrates overnight success. We see the finished product and assume it happened quickly. We do not see the years of preparation, the failed attempts, the quiet work that happened before anyone was watching. Because we do not see it, we assume we should be further along than we are.

But growth does not work that way. Progress is slow. Foundations take time. And just because you cannot see the results yet does not mean they are not coming.

I thought about everything I had been working on—the books I had written, the platform I was building, the message I was trying to share—and I realized I had everything I needed already embedded within me. The doubt wasn't about capability. It was about trust.

Did I trust the process? Did I trust that the work I was putting in would eventually pay off? Did I trust that God had given me everything I needed to succeed?

The answer was yes. I just had to keep reminding myself of that.

I approached the exit for Oconomowoc, and the hospital came into view. I thought about how doctors spend years in training before they ever perform surgery. They do not question whether they are ready. They trust the process. They trust that the preparation will equip them for the moment.

That is what I needed to do. Trust the process. Trust that the work I am doing now is building something that will matter later. Trust that even when I cannot see the progress, it is still happening.

I passed Mile Marker 282.8 and exhaled. The doubt was still there, but it was quieter now because I had decided to trust God's faithfulness, not my own ability. He has never failed me, not in separation from my loved ones, not when I felt I wasn't smart enough, not even when everything in life seemed to be against me. I held onto that same promise, believing He is not going to start now.

So here is my encouragement to you: if you are in a season where you are questioning everything, pause. Trust the process. Trust that the work you are doing matters. Trust that the seeds you are planting will grow. You have everything you need already within you. Now it is a matter of trusting the process and staying the course because we are never alone.

***Trust the process. You have everything you need within you.***

# DAY 44

## Mile Marker 289.4: The Journey to Key West

*"Endurance isn't about avoiding discomfort. It's about finishing what you started."*
LIFE LESSON

Sitting in my hotel room in Fort Lauderdale I stared at the GPS on my phone. Key West was three and a half hours south. Three and a half hours there. Three and a half hours back. Seven hours total in the car for a trip I wasn't even sure I wanted to take.

The doubt started creeping in immediately. That's a long drive. What if the traffic is bad? What if it's not worth it? What if I get halfway there and regret it? But I'd already made the decision. I was going.

The next morning, I got in the car and started driving. The highway stretched out ahead of me, long and flat, cutting through the Florida Keys. Water on both sides. Bridges connecting small islands. The sun was bright, and the air smelled like salt.

About halfway there, I almost turned around. I was tired. The drive was longer than I expected. I started questioning why I had committed to this in the first place. What was I trying to prove? Who was I doing this for?

Then I realized something: the journey back was the same distance as the journey forward. If I turned around now, I would still have to drive three and a half hours. I wouldn't save any time. I wouldn't avoid the effort. I would just miss the destination.

I thought about how often we do this in life. We start something with excitement—a goal, a dream, a commitment—and halfway through, when it gets hard, we want to quit. We tell ourselves it's not worth it, that it's taking too long, that maybe we made a mistake. But quitting doesn't make it easier. It just means we walked away before we got to see the result.

I kept driving. Past Marathon. Past Big Pine Key. Past all the little islands that make up the stretch to Key West. And when I finally arrived, I understood why

I had come. It wasn't just about the destination. It was about proving to myself that I could finish what I started, that I could endure discomfort for the sake of something meaningful.

The southernmost point of the United States. A marker that said I had been there. I had done it. I had completed the journey.

As I stood there looking out at the water, I thought about all the goals I've set this year—the ones that feel too big, the ones that require endurance, the ones that make me question if I have what it takes. And I realized the only way to get there is to keep going.

Your journey isn't meant to be easy. It is meant to build you, to test your commitment, to show you what you're made of. So, if you're halfway through something and you're thinking about turning around, don't. The journey back is the same distance as the journey forward. You might as well finish what you started.

*Endurance isn't about avoiding discomfort.*
*It's about finishing what you started.*

# DAY 45

## Mile Marker 268.2: Rejection is Favor

*"And we know that in all things God works for the good of those who love him, who have been called according to his purpose."*

ROMANS 8:28 (NIV)

Every day felt like a struggle. It was often the struggle that pulled me into negative thoughts, into thinking about what I had not accomplished, what was causing extra stress, and what I wished would just be easier. Those thoughts usually showed up on my early morning drives. It was not always deep sadness or a heavy cloud, but those drives gave me room to reflect on who I was as a professional and who I was as a person. They exposed the places where I still wrestled with self-love and self-acceptance.

One thing that has always been hard to accept is that what we are going through today can somehow work for our good later but sometimes living it out was the hard part.

This mile marker was not from my regular commute between Milwaukee and Madison. I was driving on I-41, heading to a work event. I had been publishing multiple books and trying to find my rhythm as an author and a leader. For the first time in a long time, I felt like I was in a good place. I was gaining a cadence. I knew what I needed to do, how I needed to do it, and why it mattered. I had just released, or was preparing to release, *Self-Publishing from Scratch* and I was excited. This book was intentional. It took on a real problem. It required late nights, sacrifices, and a level of discipline I had not always seen in myself. It reminded me that I was capable and that God had given me something meaningful to share.

That is why the blow hit so hard. In the middle of that momentum, one of the distribution companies decided to block my book. As I drove, the emails started coming in. Stores that had already listed my book began to pull it. One by one, those notifications felt like doors slamming shut. In a matter of hours, joy turned into confusion. I thought about the nights I stayed up writing, the energy I gave when I was already tired, and the integrity I poured into trying to help other people tell their stories. It felt unfair. It felt personal. And for a moment, it made me question why I had done all of it in the first place.

Life can feel like that. One moment you are on a clear stretch of highway, and everything seems to be going well. The next moment, something changes without warning. What felt like a blessing suddenly feels like a setback. As I drove on that highway, it did not feel like "all things working together for good." It felt like rejection. It felt like loss.

But sitting with that pain, I realized something important. Things worth having are worth fighting for. A closed door does not always mean you were wrong. Sometimes it means you have a choice to make. I could lie there in defeat, replaying those rejection emails in my mind, or I could stand up and fight for what I believed God placed in my hands. That was the other side of the coin. One side was disappointment. The other side was determination.

I chose to fight. I asked questions. I pushed for answers. I revisited my work and my process. In that fight, I discovered strength I did not know I had. I saw how much I had learned about publishing. I saw how my voice and my experience could help someone else avoid the same roadblock. That rejection became both a lesson and a mirror. It showed me that all things really can work together, even when the "all things" include rejection, confusion, and tears in the car.

Over time, I watched God redeem what felt like a dead end. *Self-Publishing from Scratch* went on to trend #1 in three categories. The very book that had been blocked became a testimony of what can happen when you keep moving, keep trusting, and keep doing the work in front of you. That mile marker on I-41 reminded me that rejection can be a form of protection, redirection, and preparation. It does not feel good in the moment, but it can lead to something greater than you imagined.

Today, you might be standing in your own version of those emails. Maybe something you worked hard for has been delayed, blocked, or taken away. Maybe you are questioning your effort, your value, or whether it is worth it to keep going. Let this be a reminder that God is still working all things together for your good. The ups and downs, the green lights and the sudden detours, the open doors and the ones that close right in your face are all seen by Him. He is not wasting your struggle he's giving it a testimony.

***Sometimes rejection is just protection in disguise.***

# DAY 46

## Mile Marker 254.8: The Weight of Comparison

*"Comparison blinds you to your own progress. Stay in your lane."*
WISDOM FOR THE JOURNEY

I was driving to work when I glanced over at the lane next to me. The cars were moving there—not fast, but steady—while my lane sat still. I watched them pass, one after another, and I felt it rising in me: frustration, impatience, the question. Why is their lane moving and mine isn't?

It's such a small thing. Traffic. Lanes. Movement. But it's a picture of something bigger.

Comparison.

We do this all the time. We look at someone else's life and feel like they're moving faster, going further, accomplishing more. And we start to wonder what's wrong with us. Why aren't I where they are? Why is their business growing and mine isn't? Why did they get the promotion, and I didn't?

The highway curved ahead, and eventually my lane started moving. And you know what happened? The lane that had been moving stopped. They hit their own delay while I kept going.

That's how life works. Everyone's journey has its own rhythm. Their lane moves now. Yours moves later. And just because you're waiting doesn't mean you're behind.

I passed a semi-truck and thought about how we only see the highlight reel. We see people's wins, their success, their movement. We don't see the delays they faced before that, the traffic they sat in, the times they questioned if they were on the right path.

Comparison steals your peace. It makes you feel like you're not doing enough, like you're falling behind, like everyone else has it figured out, and you're still struggling.

But that's a lie.

Your lane was built for you. Your timing is specific to your journey. And the progress you're making, even when it feels invisible, is still progress.

I thought about the goals I've been chasing, the things I've been working toward, and how easy it is to measure myself against someone else's pace. But their journey isn't mine. Their timeline isn't mine. And their success doesn't mean I'm failing.

I passed Mile Marker 254.8 and made a decision. I wasn't going to compare my lane to anyone else's. I was going to stay focused on where I was going and trust that my movement would come when it was supposed to.

Because comparison blurs your lane. It makes you lose sight of your own progress. And when you stop measuring yourself against someone else, you finally see how far you've actually come.

**Comparison blinds you to your own progress. Stay in your lane.**

# DAY 47

## Mile Marker 252.6: The Risk Worth Taking

*"Fear highlights the risk, but faith reveals the reward."*

TRUTH FOR COURAGE

Sitting at a red light one morning, my palms began to sweat. Not because of the traffic. Not because I was late. But because I was about to make a decision that scared me. I was about to take a risk.

The light turned green, and I pressed the gas. My mind was racing with all the what-ifs. What if this doesn't work? What if I fail? What if I lose more than I gain? But underneath all the fear was something else, a quiet whisper that said, What if it works?

I merged onto I-94 and thought about all the times I've stood at the edge of a decision, paralyzed by fear. Times I almost didn't publish a book. Times I almost didn't start a business. Times I almost didn't share my story. Every single time I chose to jump, I discovered something: the reward was greater than the fear.

The highway stretched out ahead, wide and open. I thought about the risks I've taken. Some worked out exactly how I hoped. Others didn't. Even the ones that didn't go as planned taught me something I wouldn't have learned by playing it safe. Risk will always come with fear. That's part of the process. Courage isn't about eliminating fear. It's about moving forward in spite of it.

I passed a billboard advertising a new development. "Build your dream here," it said. I thought about how you can't build anything without risk. You can't start a business without the possibility of failure. You can't write a book without the fear that no one will read it. You can't step into your calling without the chance that you might fall. You also can't grow without taking the leap.

I thought about the people who play it safe. Who stay in jobs they hate because it's comfortable. Who hold onto dreams but never act on them because the risk feels too big. Who live their whole lives wondering what could have been. I made a decision. I would rather fail trying than succeed at playing small.

The exit for Delafield came into view, and I exhaled. The fear was still there, but it didn't control me anymore. I had chosen to trust that the risk was worth it.

So, here's my encouragement to you: if there is a risk you've been avoiding, take it. Don't let fear keep you stuck. Don't let the possibility of failure stop you from trying. The leap is what will grow you. Often, the reward is greater than the fear.

***Fear highlights the risk, but faith reveals the reward.***

# DAY 48

## Mile Marker 302.6: Consistency Builds Character

*"Success is built in the small steps you repeat when no one is watching."*
PRINCIPLE OF EXCELLENCE

The highway looked the same this morning as it did yesterday. And the day before that. Same route. Same exits. Same mile markers passing one at a time. It wasn't exciting. It wasn't glamorous. It was just consistent.

As I drove, I thought about how success works the same way. We celebrate the big moments—the launches, the breakthroughs, the wins everyone sees. But those moments don't happen without the quiet, unglamorous work no one notices.

The daily grind. The small steps. The commitment to keep going even when it feels like nothing is changing. I passed a construction site where a building was going up. The workers were there again, like they had been every morning for weeks. Laying brick. Pouring concrete. Building slowly, one piece at a time.

They weren't done yet. The building didn't look impressive. But they were showing up. Consistently. And eventually, all those small efforts would add up to something significant.

That's what consistency does. It builds. Slowly. Steadily. Without fanfare. I thought about my own journey—the books I've written, the content I've created, the goals I've been working toward. None of it happened overnight. It happened because I kept showing up. Day after day. Week after week. Even when I didn't feel like it. Even when no one was watching.

Consistency taught me discipline. It showed me that keeping promises to myself builds confidence. It reminded me that the effort still matters, even when the applause is silent.

I passed Mile Marker 302.6 and thought about all the people who start strong but don't finish. Who have big dreams but lack the discipline to see them through. Who get excited about the idea but lose momentum when the work gets hard.

I realized consistency separates those who succeed from those who don't. Success isn't about the big leaps. It's about the small steps you repeat when no one is watching. It's showing up to write even when you don't feel inspired. It's working on your business even when the sales are slow. It's investing in your health even when the results aren't visible yet.

The truth is, consistency is a quiet builder. It won't always feel glamorous. You won't always see immediate results. But over time, it will shape you. It will build habits. It will build trust. And most importantly, it will build character.

I pulled into the parking lot at work and turned off the engine. Another day. Another drive. Another opportunity to be consistent.

And that's enough

**Success is built in the small steps you repeat when no one is watching.**

# DAY 49

## Mile Marker 253.6: The Pivot from Pain

*"Pain is not always punishment. Sometimes it's the pivot toward purpose."*

PERSPECTIVE SHIFT

I was driving through a storm. The rain was coming down so hard I could barely see the road ahead. My wipers were on full speed, and I'd slowed to a crawl, trying to navigate the downpour.

All I could think was, This wasn't supposed to happen. I had plans. A timeline. A vision for how things were supposed to go. But life had other ideas. Pain showed up uninvited, and it disrupted everything. The disappointment. The betrayal. The loss. It hit me hard, and for a while, I let it consume me. I thought pain was the end of the story.

Somewhere between the rain and the road, I realized something: pain doesn't have to be the end. It can be the pivot.

I thought about all the times pain forced me to move in directions I never would have chosen on my own. It closed doors I didn't want to leave behind. It stripped away things I thought I needed. In the middle of that loss, it opened new doors too—doors I wouldn't have seen if I hadn't been forced to turn around.

The rain started to let up, and I could see the road ahead a little clearer. I thought about how pain gave me new strength, how it grew compassion in me, how it revealed clarity about who I was and what I was capable of. I wouldn't have chosen it, but I can't deny what it produced.

Pain stripped away my pride. It humbled me. It taught me to lean on God in ways I never had before. In that dependence, I found a strength I didn't know I had.

I passed a sign for Lake Mills, and the sun began to break through the clouds. Light was coming. The storm was passing. I realized pain doesn't last forever. It feels permanent in the moment. It feels like it will never end. But it does. On the other side, there is growth you wouldn't have experienced any other way.

I thought about the people who let pain break them—who get stuck in bitterness, resentment, or defeat—and I understood why. Pain is heavy. It's hard to carry. It can feel easier to sit in it than to push through it. I also thought about the people who let pain pivot them—who took what hurt and used it as fuel, who turned their mess into a message, who allowed their struggle to become their strength.

I made a decision. I wasn't going to let pain break me. I was going to let it build me.

I passed Mile Marker 253.6, and the storm was behind me. The road ahead was clear.

***Pain is not always punishment. Sometimes it's the pivot toward purpose.***

# DAY 50

## Mile Marker 298.6: Embracing Reality

*"Stop pretending. Embrace your reality. God works best in truth."*

FREEDOM IN HONESTY

As I get older, I find myself sitting in my car before and after work more often, staring at my phone. Social media was full of people posting their wins, their highlights, and their best moments. And I felt the pressure to do the same. To post something that made my life look perfect. To pretend everything was fine. To put on the mask that says, "I've got it all together." But I didn't.

I started the car and pulled onto the highway. The morning was gray, and the road felt heavy. I thought about how much energy we spend pretending. Performing strength when we're barely holding on. Acting like we're fine when we're falling apart. And I realized pretending doesn't lighten the load. It just hides it.

The truth is, challenges will come. Life will shake us. It won't always feel fair. But here's what I've learned: it's not the end of the world. It might be the beginning of a deeper strength.

That day, two words kept circling my mind: honesty and endurance. Honesty first. How rare it feels. How we've been conditioned to hide our struggles instead of owning them. We call vulnerability weakness when it is one of the bravest choices we can make. What if we gave ourselves permission to admit, "I'm not okay right now"? Imagine the pressure that would lift if we stopped performing strength and allowed ourselves to be human.

Then endurance. Life is not only about living; it is about lasting. It is learning to weather the storm and step out on the other side with a steadier heart. Endurance changes us. We grow. And the quiet blessing of it is looking back and saying, "I made it through that," and knowing you can make it through what comes next

I passed Mile Marker 298.6, and the sun started to break through the clouds. I thought about the danger of getting stuck wishing life looked different, of ignoring the reality right in front of us. Reality has a way of waking us up, telling the truth, and if we let it, helping us change.

Change is uncomfortable. It's hard. It asks us to face what we would rather avoid. But it is a gift. Without reality, we stay stuck in illusion. And illusion doesn't produce growth.

I pulled into the parking lot at work and sat for a moment. I wasn't going to pretend today. I wasn't going to perform. I was going to embrace my reality, even if it was messy. Because God works best in truth, not performance. And when you face your reality with honesty, you find the strength you didn't know you had.

***Stop pretending. Embrace your reality. God works best in truth.***

# DAY 51

## Mile Marker 299.4: The Permission to Be Real

*"Embracing reality is the first step toward real growth."*

PATH TO AUTHENTICITY

I was on my way to a leadership meeting, and my mind was racing. I was thinking about what I wanted to say, how I wanted to present myself, and what impression I wanted to leave. Underneath all of that was a question: Am I being real, or am I performing?

The highway was busy, full of people heading to their own destinations. I thought about how we all wear masks, how we show up as the version of ourselves we think people want to see instead of who we actually are. And I wondered what would happen if we just stopped.

I passed a billboard that said, "Be yourself. Everyone else is taken." I smiled. It is such a simple truth, but we forget it constantly. We convince ourselves that we have to maintain an image, that we have to be strong all the time, that showing struggle is weakness.

But that is a lie.

The truth is, challenges will come. There will always be something that shakes us. It is not the end of the world. And pretending it is not happening does not make it go away.

What if we became more comfortable admitting when things are not okay? What if we let people see the real us, not just the highlight reel?

I thought about leadership. We often think being a good leader means having all the answers, never showing doubt, always being confident. But the best leaders I know are the ones who are real. They admit when they do not know. They are honest about their struggles. They lead from authenticity instead of performance.

I passed the exit for Delafield and thought about the meeting I was heading to. I made a decision. I was not going to perform today. I was going to be real.

Life is not just about living. It is about enduring. When we endure honestly, we grow in ways we never could by pretending.

So here is my challenge to you: give yourself permission to be real. Stop pretending you have it all together. Stop performing strength when you need rest. Stop hiding your reality because you think it is not acceptable. God works best in truth. When you face your reality with honesty, you will find a strength you did not know you had.

***Embracing reality is the first step toward real growth.***

# DAY 52

## Mile Marker 292.2: Questions You Need to Ask

*"Knowing your assignment means saying no to everything that isn't it."*

CLARITY OF PURPOSE

My mind often wanders driving home from work. This time I was thinking about all the things I'd accomplished, all the goals I'd set, all the wins I'd celebrated. But underneath all of that was a nagging feeling, a question I couldn't shake: Am I doing what I'm supposed to be doing?

The highway was quiet, and the sun was setting behind me. I thought about purpose, about calling, about the difference between being busy and being intentional. I passed Mile Marker 292.2 and thought about all the activity in my life—the meetings, the projects, the commitments. I was doing a lot. But was I doing the right things?

There's a difference between motion and progress, between being busy and being purposeful. Somewhere along the way, I had confused the two. I thought about a conversation I had with myself weeks ago, the one where God asked me a simple question: What is your assignment? Not what do you want to do. Not what looks good. Not what other people expect. What is your assignment?

The fields on either side of the highway were dark now, barely visible in the fading light. I thought about how easy it is to get distracted, to chase opportunities that look good but aren't aligned with your calling, to say yes to things that fill your calendar but don't fulfill your purpose. And I realized I had been doing exactly that. I had been so focused on doing more that I stopped asking if I was doing what mattered most.

The truth is, we can be successful at the wrong things. We can build a life that looks impressive from the outside but feels empty on the inside. We can climb the ladder only to realize we placed it against the wrong wall. I passed a church on the right, and the lights were on inside. I thought about how clarity comes in the quiet, how God speaks when we stop moving long enough to listen, how purpose is revealed when we're willing to ask the hard questions.

What is my assignment? Not what can I do, but what am I supposed to do?

I thought about all the things I had said yes to that weren't part of my assignment—the commitments that drained me, the projects that pulled me away from my core calling, the opportunities that looked good but weren't God-directed. And I realized that saying yes to everything means saying no to the one thing that matters most.

I pulled into my driveway and sat in the car for a moment. The question was still there, sitting heavy in my spirit. I knew I needed to answer it honestly. What is my assignment? Not tomorrow. Not when I have more time. Not when everything else is finished. Now. Because until I get clear on what I'm supposed to be doing, I'll keep spinning my wheels doing everything else.

So, here's my challenge to you: ask yourself the same question. What is your assignment? Not what are you capable of. Not what looks impressive. Not what other people think you should do. What has God assigned you to do? And once you get the answer, have the courage to let go of everything else.

***Knowing your assignment means saying no to everything that isn't it.***

# DAY 53

## Mile Marker 271.4: Guard Your Lane

*"Let your eyes look straight ahead; fix your gaze directly before you."*
PROVERBS 4:25 (NIV)

This morning, I left the house a little later than usual. Instead of my normal 6:30 a.m. departure, I headed toward Madison closer to eight. The sky was clear, the road was familiar, and my plan was simple. I wanted to get a few things done in the office, be present with my team, and show my face after being away for a few days.

At first, the highway moved like it always did. Cars flowed smoothly, and I settled into my lane. As I drew closer to Mile Marker 271.4, I noticed that traffic started to slow down. Brake lights lit up in front of me, and before long we were creeping along.

My first thought was, "What is going on up there?" Maybe someone had a flat tire. Maybe there was some debris in the road. Maybe there was an accident. As I inched forward, I finally saw it. A sheriff had a car pulled over on the shoulder. There was no lane closure. No emergency vehicles blocking the road. Just one car and one officer handling their business on the side of the highway.

Yet for miles, everyone had tapped their brakes. People were staring out their windows, trying to see what was happening. And right in the middle of that slow crawl, I found myself saying out loud, "Why do we keep doing this? The sheriff is not leaving that car to come chase us. They are already handling something else."

As I drove on, it struck me how much that moment looked like life. So often, the situation someone else is dealing with has nothing to do with us, but we still slow down our own journey to study it. We become distracted by their consequences. We wonder what they did. We replay their choices. We add our opinions, assumptions, and judgments, all while the lane in front of us waits for our attention.

That morning, I had a nine o'clock meeting. The delay caused by everyone watching what did not involve them pushed back my timing. Their curiosity cost all of us time.

Life can be the same way. When we spend our energy staring at someone else's struggle, success, or discipline, we risk missing what God is trying to do in us. The more we fix our eyes on another person's lane, the easier it is to drift in our own. And sometimes, our drifting does not just affect us. It creates delays, detours, and frustration for the people behind us who are simply trying to reach where they need to go.

Looking back on that drive, I realized I needed the reminder. I do not have to carry the weight of somebody else's moment on the shoulder of life. I have my own assignment, my own responsibilities, and my own destination to reach. My job is to pay attention to what is in front of me.

When we stay focused on what is in front of us, we honor the assignment God has given us and we move with a lot more peace. The moment we start staring at what is happening in someone else's lane, we can drift, slow down, and unintentionally affect the people who are following behind us.

I want to invite you to pay attention to where you might be "rubbernecking" in your own life. Are there places where you have slowed your progress to study someone else's drama, decisions, or discipline? Maybe it shows up in comparison. Maybe it shows up in replaying a situation that does not involve you. What would it look like today to bring your eyes back to what God has placed in front of you and give that your best energy?

You might even whisper a simple prayer: "Lord, thank You for giving me a lane, an assignment, and a destination. Help me to keep my eyes on what You have placed in front of me. Teach me not to slow down my journey trying to carry what does not belong to me. Give me wisdom to pray for others and still stay faithful in my lane. Amen." It's in these types of moments when we allow God to take control and steer our journey.

***Our responsibility in life is to pay attention to the lane we are driving in to prevent detours and delays for others.***

# DAY 54

## Mile Marker 248.6: The Mirror Never Lies

*"Time is sacred. Honor it by living fully, not just existing."*
VALUE OF THE MOMENT

Running late again this morning, rushing through my daily routine, I caught myself standing in the mirror. Not moving. Just standing there, thinking. I had been dealing with the loss of loved ones lately—trying to juggle life, expectations, and priorities. Trying to keep it all together while pieces of my heart were missing. In that moment, staring at my own reflection, something hit me hard.

Even in our deepest pain, life does not pause. I looked out the window and realized it was true. The world does not stop. It keeps spinning without hesitation. Cars were still moving down the road. People were still waiting at the bus stop. And ladybugs were still finding their way into my house. Life keeps moving, even when we feel stuck.

I finally pulled myself together, made it to the car, and started driving. The highway was busy with people heading to their own destinations, carrying their own weight. I thought about how we spend our time. How we waste it holding on to things long past their purpose—arguments we cannot let go of, regret over what we cannot change, old pain we rehearse like it is new, missed opportunities we mourn instead of learning from. We tell ourselves, "I'll deal with it later," not realizing that later is not promised.

On that drive, near Mile Marker 248.6, three truths surfaced that I had to confront.

Truth one: Time is sacred. It is not something you manage. It is something you honor. Stop giving your peace to things that drain you. If it does not grow you, free you, or align with your purpose, let it go.

Truth two: Healing is not forgetting. It is remembering differently. It is choosing to carry love over bitterness, legacy over loss. The people we have lost do not want us living stuck in grief. They want us living full.

Truth three: The mirror never lies. When you look at your reflection, ask yourself, Am I truly living, or just existing? You cannot get these moments back, and what you do with them matters.

The highway stretched ahead, and I realized grief is love with nowhere to go. But it does not have to paralyze you. It can propel you. It can remind you that time is precious. So maybe it is time to recenter, reevaluate, and reclaim your life with intention.

Stop waiting for the perfect moment to heal. Stop existing when you were created to live. The mirror never lies. And when you look at yourself today, make sure you see someone who is living.

***Honor your legacy by living fully instead of merely existing.***

# DAY 55

## Mile Marker 251.8: Stand in the Uncomfortable

*"Go stand in the place where you feel uncomfortable until you're there long enough that it isn't."*

RYAN COOGLER

On the drive to work one morning, I stumbled across an interview with Ryan Coogler and heard him say something that stopped me in my tracks: "Go stand in the place where you feel uncomfortable until you're there long enough that it isn't." I replayed it. Let it sit. Let it settle into the places I had been avoiding. And it hit me hard.

The highway stretched ahead, familiar and predictable, but that thought wasn't. I had driven this route thousands of times. I knew every exit, every curve, every landmark. There was comfort in that. Safety. No surprises. But comfort doesn't produce growth. I thought about the places that scare me, the ones that make me hesitate, second-guess, or feel like I am not enough. The opportunities I talked myself out of because they felt too big, too risky, too different from where I am now. And I realized those places are often exactly where I am supposed to be.

Growth never happens in the comfort zone. It happens in the stretch, in the risk, in the reach. I passed a construction site where a new building was going up. The workers weren't comfortable. They were climbing scaffolding, operating heavy machinery, working in conditions that required focus and courage. But they were building something.

That is what standing in the uncomfortable does. It builds you. It stretches you. It forces you to become the version of yourself that is capable of handling what you couldn't before. I thought about all the things I have been avoiding—starting the project that feels too ambitious, having the conversation that feels too vulnerable, pursuing the dream that feels too uncertain. And I asked myself the same question I am asking you: What have you been talking yourself out of because it felt too big?

Maybe it is starting the business. Maybe it is going back to school. Maybe it is finally speaking your truth. Whatever it is, stop waiting to feel ready. Stop waiting for fear to disappear. It won't. Do it anyway.

The version of you on the other side of that fear is stronger, wiser, freer. But you will never meet that version if you stay where it is comfortable. So today, I am challenging you: stand in that uncomfortable place. Let it mold you. Let it stretch you. Stay there until the discomfort fades. Stay there until it isn't uncomfortable anymore.

You were made for more. Don't let comfort rob you of calling.

***Stand in the uncomfortable long enough,
and it stops being uncomfortable.***

# DAY 56

## Mile Marker 252.4: Stop Listening to Them

*"Your vision doesn't need their approval. It just needs your obedience."*
TRUTH FOR DREAMERS

God seems to always know when to speak to me on my morning commutes. This morning, just outside Lake Mills, a thought dropped into my spirit—clear, direct, unshakable: Stop listening to them.

Not to a specific person, but to all of them. The voices that question your vision. The people who cannot see what you see. The ones who think your dream is too big, too risky, too unrealistic.

While the highway was busy, full of people heading in different directions, I thought about how easy it is to let other people's opinions dictate your path. In that moment, truth rose up: they do not need to see your vision. It was not given to them. It was given to you. They do not need to understand it. They do not need to agree with it. They do not need to approve it. Yet we keep handing our purpose to people who were never qualified to hold it.

I passed Pewaukee, and the lake was calm. I thought about how still water reflects what is above it, but if you throw a stone in, the reflection gets distorted. That is what happens when you let other people's opinions disrupt your vision. The clarity you had gets muddied by their doubt.

I thought about all the times I have second-guessed myself because someone did not believe in what I was building. How I edited my dreams to make them more palatable. How I dimmed my vision to fit their understanding. And I realized I was giving them power they never deserved.

Your calling does not need their permission. Your purpose does not require their approval. What God planted in you is not subject to their validation.

So today, take it back. Take back your dream. Take back your vision. Take back the boldness that someone's doubt tried to steal. Trust what God put inside you. Trust your process. Trust that small whisper that keeps telling you, There's more for me. Because there is.

I thought about Moses. How God called him to lead, and he immediately listed reasons he could not. How he looked at his inadequacies instead of God's ability. God did not ask for his résumé. He gave him an assignment.

The same is true for you. God did not plant a dream in you that requires everyone else's approval. He planted it because He already approved it. So, stop listening to them. Stop waiting for permission. Start believing in yourself. And go make it happen.

***Your vision doesn't need their approval. It just needs your obedience.***

# DAY 57

## Mile Marker 284.4: Today is a New Day

*"Yesterday is over. Today is yours. Don't let the past steal your present."*
DAILY RENEWAL

I woke up this morning still carrying yesterday. The conversation that didn't go well. The decision that threw me off. The thing I said that I wish I could take back. By the time I got in the car, I was replaying it all, rewinding moments I couldn't change, letting yesterday bleed into today like it had permission to be here.

It took a little time to get on the highway because everyone seemed to be driving slowly. When I finally did, it was quiet, and the sun was just starting to rise. The sky was painted in soft shades of pink and gold, and everything looked new. Fresh. Like the earth reset itself overnight. And I thought, why can't I do the same?

Maybe yesterday wasn't the best day for you. Someone said something that disrupted your peace. A decision was made that changed how you felt. Someone upset you, or maybe you did something you are not proud of. But today, you have been given a new day.

I passed Brookfield, and the morning dew still clung to the grass. Everything looked clean, untouched, like yesterday's mess had been wiped away while we slept. That is what today is. A reset. A fresh start. A chance to let go of what did not go right and focus on what still can.

We do not always see it that way. We wake up defeated because something went wrong yesterday. We carry the weight of disappointment as if it were permanent. We let one bad moment define the next twenty-four hours. Don't allow yesterday's failures to dictate today's successes.

That mistake you made is done. That conversation that went sideways is over. That decision you regret cannot be undone. But you can choose how you move forward.

I thought about God's mercies. They are new every morning. Not because we earned them, but because He knows we need them. He does not wake us up and remind us of everything we got wrong yesterday. He gives us a clean slate. So why do we hold on to what He has already released?

Take your power back. Do not give yesterday permission to steal today. Do not let someone else's words or actions control how you show up right now. Today is yours. Make it count.

***Yesterday is over. Today is yours. Don't let the past steal your present.***

# DAY 58

## Mile Marker 276.4: Allow Life to Be Life

*"Be still, and know that I am God."*

PSALM 46:10 (NIV)

Today I was driving along the highway. It was a Wednesday morning, and I was in the left lane. The temperature had dropped, so I was back to wearing suit jackets. The trees were beginning to lose their leaves, the grass was turning brown, and the air felt crisp.

As I looked ahead, the sky was completely clear. Not a single cloud in sight. It was about eight o'clock in the morning, and a full moon was perfectly positioned above the tree line. For a moment, I just stared in awe.

It made me think about life. How every day we move through our routines without realizing we are just a small fragment of something much larger. We live on a planet filled with billions of moving parts, all happening at once. I was one car on one highway, but there were thousands of others around the world. And above it all, that same moon hovered, a reminder that beyond this earth there are other planets and galaxies still unfolding.

Sometimes we forget how big life really is. The situations we face and the problems we carry feel heavy, yet in the grand scheme they are small. The world keeps moving. Birds take flight, mosquitoes fade with the season, trees release their leaves, and the weather shifts. It is all part of a cycle we cannot control.

So why do we try so hard to control everything about our days instead of existing in the moment?

I thought about all the energy I spend trying to manage outcomes. Trying to force doors open that are not ready. Trying to make things happen on my timeline instead of trusting the natural rhythm of life.

The moon does not rush across the sky. The trees do not stress about when to release their leaves. The seasons do not apologize for changing. They simply are.

Maybe that was the lesson I needed today. To stop fighting against the flow of life and allow it to unfold. To trust that just as the moon rises and sets, just as the seasons change without my permission, my life is moving exactly as it should.

I passed Mile Marker 276.4 and exhaled. The moon was still there, steady and unhurried. I realized I do not have to control everything. I can trust that life knows what it is doing.

So here is my encouragement to you: stop trying to control every outcome. Stop forcing things that are not ready. Stop stressing over timelines that are not yours to dictate. Allow life to be life. Trust the process. Trust the rhythm. Trust that you are exactly where you need to be, even when it does not feel like it.

Because the same God who keeps the moon in the sky and changes the seasons is the same God holding your life together.

***Allow life to be life.***

# DAY 59

## Mile Marker 265.8: The Pruning Season

*"I am the true vine, and my Father is the gardener. He cuts off every branch in me that bears no fruit, while every branch that does bear fruit he prunes so that it will be even more fruitful."*

JOHN 15:1-2 (NIV)

I was driving past Delafield when I noticed something. The trees along the highway were being pruned. Workers in orange vests were cutting away dead branches, trimming back overgrowth, shaping the trees for the next season.

I thought about how painful pruning looks from the outside. If you did not know what was happening, you might think they were hurting the trees. Cutting away parts that looked fine. Removing branches that still had life in them. But pruning is not about destruction. It is about direction. It is removing what is no longer necessary so the tree can focus its energy on what matters most.

I passed the HomeGoods and thought about my own life, about the season I was in. I realized God was pruning me. He was cutting away relationships that had run their course, opportunities that looked good but were not aligned with my calling, commitments that were draining me instead of filling me.

And it hurt. Not because those things were bad, but because I had grown attached to them. I had built my identity around some of them. I had convinced myself I needed them to be whole. But God knew better. He knew that if I kept holding on to everything, I would not have the capacity to grow into what He was calling me to become.

The highway opened up ahead, and I thought about gardens. Gardeners do not prune to punish. They prune to produce. They remove the dead weight so the plant can focus its nutrients on what will bloom. That is what God was doing in my life. Removing dead weight. Cutting away distractions. Clearing space for new growth. Even though it hurt, I knew it was necessary.

I thought about the people I had to release. Not because they were toxic, but because our season together had ended. The projects I had to let go of. Not because they were bad ideas, but because they were not my assignment. The habits I had to break. Not because they were destroying me, but because they kept me comfortable when God was calling me to grow.

Pruning is uncomfortable. It feels like loss. But on the other side is growth you could not have experienced any other way.

I passed Mile Marker 265.8 and thought about next spring. Those trees will bloom fuller because of the pruning happening now. The branches that were cut away will make room for new life. That is what God is doing in me. Even though I cannot see it yet, I trust that the pruning is preparation for something better.

So here is my encouragement to you: if you are in a season where God is removing things from your life, do not resist it. Do not try to hold on to what He is trying to release. Trust the process. Trust that He is making room for something new. Trust that the pruning is preparing you for the next level of growth.

***Pruning feels like loss, but it's preparation for greater growth.***

# DAY 60

## Mile Marker 289.2: The Power of Silence

*"Silence isn't empty. It's where God speaks."*

LISTENING HEART

This morning, my playlist was ready before I was. I had a whole lineup of songs queued up—motivational tracks, worship music, things to set the tone for the day. But when I got in the car, I didn't press play. I just drove in silence.

In that stillness, I heard something I had been missing: clarity.

I have spent so much time filling the silence. Music. Podcasts. Phone calls. Anything to keep my mind occupied. Anything to avoid being alone with my thoughts. Somewhere near Pewaukee, I realized silence isn't empty. It is full. It is where God speaks. It is where ideas are born. It is where truth rises to the surface without all the noise pushing it back down.

I passed a church on the right that I had watched being built over many drives on that stretch of highway, and I thought about prayer. How often we treat it like a monologue. We talk at God, listing our requests, concerns, and needs. But we do not stop long enough to listen. We fill the space with our words and then wonder why we do not hear His.

The truth is, God speaks in the quiet. In the moments when we stop performing and start listening. In the stillness when we are willing to sit with what is uncomfortable instead of drowning it out.

I thought about the decisions I had been wrestling with. The questions I had been carrying. The direction I had been seeking. I realized I had been asking God for answers while refusing to be quiet long enough to hear them.

I passed Nagawicka Lake, it was still, like glass, reflecting the sky perfectly because there was no disruption on the surface. That is what happens when we are still. We reflect on what is true instead of what is chaotic.

I thought about how much wisdom I have missed because I was too busy talking to listen. How many times God was trying to guide me, but I could not hear Him over the noise I created. Silence is not something to fear. It is something to lean into. In the quiet, you hear what the noise has been covering. You see what the distraction has been hiding. You receive what the busyness has been blocking.

I passed Mile Marker 289.2 and made a commitment. I was going to create more space for silence, not just in the car but in my life. Moments where I was not filling the space with noise. Where I was present. Where I was listening. God does not shout over the chaos. He whispers in the quiet. If I want to hear Him, I have to be still enough to listen.

***Silence isn't empty. It's where God speaks.**ABC*

# DAY 61

## Mile Marker 269.4: The Gift of Today

*"Today is the only moment you're guaranteed. Don't waste it planning for tomorrow."*

LIVE PRESENT

The alarm went off this morning, and my first thought was about everything I had to do. The meetings. The deadlines. The tasks piling up. My mind was already racing before my feet even hit the floor. By the time I got in the car, I was thinking about tomorrow, next week, and the future I was trying to build.

Somewhere near Delafield, a thought stopped me: What if today is all I have? Not in a morbid way. Not in a fearful way. In a realistic one. The truth is, tomorrow isn't promised. We make plans like we are guaranteed another day, but we are not. Life is fragile, and the only moment we truly have is this one.

I passed a field where the morning dew still clung to the grass. The sun was just starting to touch it, making everything sparkle. It was beautiful, and I almost missed it because I was too focused on what was ahead. How many moments like this have I missed?

I thought about all the time I spend planning for the future—saving for retirement, building for tomorrow, working toward goals that are years away. None of that is wrong. Planning is wise. Preparation is important. But not at the expense of missing today.

I thought about people who spend their whole lives planning for a future they never get to experience. Who retire and do not live long enough to enjoy it. Who sacrifice the present for a tomorrow that never comes. I realized life is a gift. Not tomorrow. Today.

The highway stretched out ahead, and I thought about the people I love. The conversations I have been putting off. The moments I have been too busy to enjoy. The experiences I delayed because I thought I would have time later. But what if I do not? What if today is the last chance I have to tell someone I love them, to make that memory, to be present for that moment?

I passed Mile Marker 269.4 and made a decision. I was not going to live in tomorrow anymore. I was going to live in today. Not recklessly. Not without planning. With presence. With intention. With the awareness that this moment is the only one I am guaranteed.

So here is my encouragement to you: stop waiting for the perfect time. Stop putting off the things that matter. Stop living in a future that may never come. Be present today. Love hard today. Make the memory today. Have the conversation today. Because today is all you have, and it is a gift you do not want to waste.

*Today is the only moment you're guaranteed.*
*Don't waste it planning for tomorrow.*

# DAY 62

## Mile Marker 298.4: The Weight of Perfection

*"Done is better than perfect. Release what's ready."*

OVERCOMING PERFECTIONISM

On the way to work, my mind was on a project I'd been working on. Something I'd poured hours into. Something I believed in. But I hadn't released it yet. It wasn't ready, and for some reason, I didn't think it was perfect.

I kept revising. Tweaking. Adjusting. Trying to get it to a place where I wouldn't be criticized. Where no one could find fault. Where it would be flawless. Somewhere near Johnson Creek, I realized I was chasing something that doesn't exist.

Perfection is a myth. It's a standard we create to protect ourselves from judgment. A bar we set impossibly high, so we never have to risk putting ourselves out there. In chasing perfection, we miss the point. The point isn't to be flawless. It's to be faithful.

I passed a construction site where a building was going up. It wasn't perfect. The edges were rough. The structure was exposed. It was a work in progress. But it was progress. And I realized that's what my work was meant to be. Not perfect. But progressing.

I thought about all the projects I'd delayed because they weren't perfect yet. The ideas I'd shelved because I was afraid of criticism. The dreams I'd held back because I didn't think I was ready. I saw how I was letting perfection rob me of momentum.

The truth is, done is better than perfect. Perfect never ships. Perfect never launches. Perfect stays hidden in the safety of almost, never risking the exposure of actually.

I passed the Pine Cone restaurant and thought about the people waiting for what I'm holding back. The ones who need to hear the message I'm afraid to share. The ones who would benefit from the work I'm too scared to release. My fear of imperfection was keeping them from what they needed.

That's selfish. Not intentionally. But the result is the same. When I hold back out of fear, I'm withholding what someone else is waiting for.

I passed Mile Marker 298.4 and made a decision. I was going to release the project. Not when it was perfect, but when it was ready. And ready doesn't mean flawless. It means it's done enough to serve its purpose.

So, here's my encouragement to you: stop waiting for perfect. It's not coming. Release what's ready. Share what's done. Put it out there, even if it's imperfect. Someone is waiting for it, and fear of criticism shouldn't keep them from what they need.

***Done is better than perfect. Release what's ready.***

# DAY 63

## Mile Marker 244.4: The Reset Button

*"Every morning is a reset. Let yesterday go and step into today."*
FRESH MERCY

It was a rough day at work. The kind of day where nothing went right. Every conversation felt off. Every task took longer than it should have. By the time I got in the car, I was carrying all of it with me—the frustration, the disappointment, the weight of a day that didn't go the way I wanted.

The highway was busy, full of people heading home from their own rough days. I thought about how easy it is to carry yesterday's weight into today, to let one bad moment define the next twenty-four hours.

Somewhere near Lake Mills, I saw something that shifted my perspective. I looked in my rearview mirror and noticed the sun setting, painting the sky in shades of orange and pink. I realized the day was ending. The sky was resetting. Tomorrow, it would rise again—fresh and new.

That's what God does. Every morning, He gives us a reset. We don't earn it, and we don't deserve it, but because He knows we need it, He gives it. What an amazing gift—His mercy is new every morning. God doesn't hold our yesterday against us. He gives us another chance, even when we don't deserve it. In that moment, I centered myself and said, "If God is willing to reset, why am I holding on to what's already done?"

The truth is, we sabotage our tomorrows by clinging to our yesterdays. We let bad days bleed into good ones. We let disappointment define our next opportunity. We let failure convince us we can't try again. That's not how God operates. He gives us a reset. A fresh start. A clean slate. All we have to do is accept it.

Holding on to yesterday doesn't honor it. It just keeps you from moving forward.

Passing Mile Marker 244.4, I made a decision. I wasn't going to carry today into tomorrow. I wasn't going to let this rough day steal my peace or my focus. I was going to accept the reset, let it go, and trust that tomorrow would be better.

Because God gives us new mercy every morning. And if He's willing to let yesterday go, so am I.

***Every morning is a reset. Let yesterday go and step into today.***

# DAY 64

## Mile Marker 250.8: The Voices You Listen To

*"Not every voice speaking wisdom is speaking wisdom for you. Protect what you listen to."*

DISCERNMENT IN NOISE

Sitting in traffic, a voice came on the radio giving advice about success—about building, about making it—and something about the tone felt off. The advice wasn't bad, but it wasn't aligned with who I am. It was someone else's strategy. Someone else's path. Someone else's definition of success. I realized I had been listening to the wrong voices.

As traffic started moving again, I turned the radio off. The silence gave me space to think about all the voices I allow into my life—the podcasts, the social media influencers, the experts, the people who claim to have it all figured out. Not every voice deserves my attention.

During my drive I thought about how water reflects what is above it. If the sky is clear, the reflection is clear. If the sky is cloudy, the reflection is cloudy too. That is what happens when we listen to the wrong voices. We start reflecting on their perspective instead of our own. We start chasing their goals instead of ours. We start measuring success by their standards. And we lose ourselves in the process.

I thought about advice I had taken that did not fit, strategies I tried that did not work, and goals I chased that left me empty when I achieved them. They were not wrong, but they were not mine. The truth is, not every voice speaking wisdom is speaking wisdom for you. Not every strategy that works for someone else will work for you. Not every path that leads to success for them will lead to fulfillment for you. You have to discern which voices to listen to.

I passed a billboard advertising a conference and thought about how much noise there is in the world. Everyone has an opinion. Everyone has a method. Everyone has a blueprint for how you should live your life. But the voice that truly matters is the one inside you—the one that knows your calling, understands your assignment, and is the one God speaks through.

I passed Mile Marker 250.8 and made a commitment. I would be more selective about the voices I allow in. Not because I do not value other perspectives, but because I need to protect my own. The loudest voice should not be someone else's. It should be God's. If I fill my head with everyone else's opinions, I will not be able to hear His.

*__Not every voice speaking wisdom is speaking wisdom for you.__*
*__Protect what you listen to.__*

# DAY 65

## Mile Marker 303.2: Halfway There

*"The middle is where most people quit. But it's also where character is built. Keep going."*
ENDURANCE TEST

This morning, something hit me. I was halfway through my drive—halfway between where I started and where I was going—and I thought about how that's a picture of life. We are always in the middle of something. Halfway through a project. Halfway through a goal. Halfway through a season. In that middle space, it is easy to lose perspective. You cannot see the beginning clearly anymore, and the end still feels too far away.

The highway stretched out ahead, and I thought about how many people quit in the middle. Not because they do not have what it takes, but because the middle is hard. The excitement of starting has worn off. The reward of finishing is not visible yet. You are left with the daily grind of just showing up. That is where most people give up.

I passed a field that was in the middle of being planted. Half of it was turned over, ready for seed. The other half was still waiting. The farmer could not stop halfway. If they did, half the field would produce, and half would not. The work would be wasted. The potential would be lost.

The middle requires faith. It requires trust that the effort you are putting in will eventually produce results. It requires endurance when you cannot see progress. I thought about the goals I set at the beginning of the year—the ones that felt exciting in January and feel overwhelming now. I realized I was in the middle. Halfway through. The temptation to quit was real. But quitting in the middle means walking away from everything I have already invested. It means the work I have done up to this point was for nothing. I was not willing to do that.

I passed Mile Marker 303.2 and thought about marathons—how runners talk about hitting the wall around mile 20. Halfway can feel manageable. The wall is where your body wants to quit. The runners who finish are the ones who push through the wall, who keep moving even when everything in them wants to stop.

That is what I need to do. Keep moving. Keep showing up. Keep trusting that the finish line is closer than it feels. The truth is, the middle is where character is built. It is where you prove to yourself that you are committed. It is where the real work happens.

So, if you are in the middle of something right now, do not quit. Do not let the distance ahead discourage you. Do not let the lack of visible progress convince you it is not working. You are halfway there, which means you are closer to the end than you were to the beginning. Keep going.

*The middle is where most people quit.*
*But it's also where character is built. Keep going.*

# DAY 66

## Mile Marker 254.6: The Cost of Comfort

*"Comfort keeps you safe, but it also keeps you stuck. Choose growth."*

BREAKING FREE

Sometimes dream about the neighborhoods we want to live in. Beautiful homes. Manicured lawns. The kind of place that signals success and stability. For a moment, I felt it—the pull toward comfort, toward settling, toward choosing what is easy over what is necessary.

Passing houses that looked like those neighborhoods along the highway, I reflected on how much we sacrifice for comfort. We stick with jobs that drain us because they are secure. We stay in relationships that do not serve us because they are familiar. We avoid risks because the unknown feels scarier than the unsatisfying. Why do we do this? Do we avoid risks because the unknown seems scarier than settling for less?

I passed a sign for HomeGoods and smiled. I love that place. Walking the aisles. Looking at things, I do not need, but enjoy seeing. It is comfortable. Easy. No pressure. But if I spent all my time there, I would never build anything. I would never grow. I would never step into the uncomfortable spaces where real transformation happens.

The truth is, growth and comfort cannot coexist. You have to choose one.

I thought about the times I chose comfort over calling. The opportunities I did not pursue because they felt too risky. The dreams I shelved because they required too much sacrifice. The conversations I avoided because they made me uncomfortable. Every time I chose comfort, I chose to stay small.

The highway curved ahead, and I thought about caterpillars. They have to break out of the cocoon to become butterflies, and the struggle to get free is what strengthens their wings. If you cut the cocoon open to make it easier, the butterfly will not be able to fly. The discomfort is necessary. The struggle is part of the process. Avoiding it does not protect you. It weakens you.

I drove past the hospital in Oconomowoc and thought about surgery. Doctors cut to heal. Recovery is painful. The patient endures discomfort for the sake of long-term health. That is what growth is. It is choosing short-term discomfort for long-term gain. Comfort is choosing short-term ease at the expense of long-term potential.

I thought about the goals I set, the things I want to accomplish, and the person I am trying to become. None of it will happen if I keep choosing comfort. I have to be willing to be uncomfortable. To take risks. To have hard conversations. To do things that scare me. Because on the other side of discomfort is the version of myself I am trying to become.

I passed Mile Marker 254.6 and made a commitment. I would not choose comfort anymore. I would choose growth, even when it hurts. Comfort keeps you safe. It also keeps you stuck. I would rather be uncomfortable and growing, than comfortable and stagnant.

*Comfort keeps you safe, but it also keeps you stuck. Choose growth.*

# DAY 67

## Mile Marker 243.8: The Comparison Trap Returns

*"Comparison steals your joy. Focus on your own lane."*
STAY FOCUSED

While scrolling through social media at a red light, I saw a post from someone I went to school with. They had just closed a major deal, bought a new house, and got promoted. My first reaction was instant: Why not me?

The light turned green, and I put the phone down, but the feeling stayed. That familiar sting of comparison. That nagging question: What am I doing wrong?

Still in my thoughts, I merged onto the highway. Traffic was moving steadily, cars in every lane heading somewhere. I realized I was doing it again—comparing my lane to someone else's. I thought about how often I do this, how I look at other people's progress and feel like I am falling behind, how I measure my success against theirs and come up short.

Here is the problem with comparison: you are comparing your behind-the-scenes to their highlight reel. You see their win, not the years of work that led to it. You see their promotion, not the sacrifices they made. You see their success, not their struggles. When you compare your entire journey to their single moment, you will always feel inadequate.

Just like the Rock River on my drive—some days calm, other days choppy—but always the same river. Our journeys look different at different times. Someone else's river may look calm today. Yours may look calm tomorrow.

The truth is, comparison steals your joy. It keeps you from celebrating where you are because you are too focused on where someone else is. I thought about the progress I have made, the things I have accomplished, and the growth I have experienced. None of it felt significant because I was too busy looking at what other people had done.

My progress is not less valuable because someone else is progressing too. My wins are not smaller because someone else is winning bigger. My journey is my own. And it is enough.

I passed a billboard for a new development. The tagline read, "Build your dream here." Not someone else's dream. Yours. That is what I needed to remember. I am not building someone else's dream. I am building mine. Their timeline does not dictate my progress.

Mile Marker 243.8 came into view, and I made a decision. I would stop comparing. I would celebrate other people's wins without diminishing my own. I would focus on my lane and trust that my progress is exactly what it needs to be. Comparison is a thief. It will not steal my peace anymore.

*Comparison steals your joy. Focus on your own lane.*

# DAY 68

## Mile Marker 278.8: The Power of No

*"No is a complete sentence. Use it to protect your peace."*

HEALTHY BOUNDARIES

While I was driving, I was on a call and someone asked me to take on another project. It sounded good. It aligned with my skills. It would look great on my résumé. But something in my spirit said no.

At the most vulnerable times, things give me a sign. This time, it was a semi-truck I was passing on my right. Looking at its bed made me think about capacity. We all have limits. Saying yes to everything means saying no to the things that matter most.

I realized I had been saying yes to too many things that were not mine to carry. The truth is, no is a complete sentence. It does not need explanation. It does not need justification. It is a boundary, and boundaries are necessary for growth.

I thought about the times I said yes when I should have said no. The commitments I took on because I did not want to disappoint someone. The projects I agreed to because I felt guilty. I pursued the opportunities that looked good, even though they did not feel right. Every time I said yes to something that was not mine, I said no to something that was.

I passed a field where the crops had been harvested. The land was resting. Not producing. Not working. Just resting. I thought about how rest is not laziness. It is wisdom. It is recognizing that you cannot produce all the time. You need seasons to pause, to restore, and to prepare for the next season of growth.

Saying no creates space for rest, for focus, and for the things that truly matter. I thought about Jesus. He said no. He walked away from crowds who wanted more from Him. He prioritized His assignment over people's expectations.

If Jesus could say no, so can I. As I passed Mile Marker 278.8, I called the person back. I thanked them for thinking of me, and I said no. It felt uncomfortable, but it also felt right.

Saying no to what is not mine creates space for what is. So here is my encouragement to you: stop saying yes to everything. Stop carrying things that are not yours to carry. Stop letting guilt or obligation dictate your commitments. Learn to say no. Not with rudeness. Not with apology. With clarity.

Because no is a powerful word. And when you use it wisely, it protects your peace and your purpose.

*No is a complete sentence. Use it to protect your peace.*

# DAY 69

## Mile Marker 281.2: The Unseen Work

*"Just because you can't see progress doesn't mean it's not happening. Keep going."*
TRUST THE PROCESS

I was driving past a construction site I'd been watching for months. When it started, it was just an empty lot. Then they dug a foundation and poured concrete. For weeks, it looked like nothing was happening. But this morning, I saw it—the walls were going up, the structure was taking shape. And I realized: all that time I thought nothing was happening, something was. I just couldn't see it.

The highway stretched ahead, and I thought about how much life works this way. We do the work. We show up. We invest time and energy into something that matters, and we don't see results. So, we start to doubt. We question if it's working. We wonder if we're wasting our time.

But just because you cannot see the progress doesn't mean it isn't happening. I thought about seeds—how farmers plant them in the ground and then wait. For weeks, there has been no visible sign of growth. Under the surface, roots are forming. Life is happening. The seed is doing what it was designed to do. And one day, a sprout breaks through. Not because something suddenly started working, but because the unseen work finally became visible. That is what I needed to remember: the work I am doing matters, even when I cannot see the results yet.

I passed the hospital in Oconomowoc and thought about healing—how it happens beneath the surface before it shows on the outside. Bones knit back together in ways we cannot see. Cells regenerate in processes we do not witness. The healing is real, even when it is invisible.

I thought about all the work I have been putting in. The books I have written that haven't sold as many copies as I hoped. The content I have created that hasn't gotten the engagement I expected. The goals that feel further away than when I started. And I realized: maybe the results aren't visible yet because the roots are still forming. Maybe the foundation is still being laid. Maybe the structure is still being built beneath the surface. One day, it will break through, and everyone will see it. But just because they do not see it now doesn't mean it isn't happening.

At Mile Marker 281.2, I felt a weight lift. I do not need to see the results to trust the process. I do not need visible progress to know I am moving forward. I just need to keep showing up, keep doing the work, and keep trusting that what is happening beneath the surface will eventually break through. The unseen work is still work. And it matters.

***Just because you can't see progress doesn't mean it's not happening. Keep going.***

# DAY 70

## Mile Marker 258.2: The People Who Stay

*"The people who stay when it's hard are the ones worth keeping."*
TRUE FRIENDSHIP

On this particular morning, I was thinking about friendship, about the people who have been in my life for years, the ones who have seen me at my best and my worst, the ones who stayed when it would have been easier to leave.

The ones I didn't want to lose.

The highway was quiet, and I thought about how rare that is. Most relationships feel conditional. People show up when it is convenient and disappear when it is not. But the people who stay are different.

I passed a church on the right and thought about community. We are not designed to do life alone. We need people who will walk with us through every season, not just show up for the highlights. Everyone will celebrate with you when you are winning. Not everyone will sit with you when you are struggling. The people who do are the ones worth keeping.

I remembered a conversation with one of my best friends. She called me out on something I was doing. I did not want to hear it. It stung. She said it because she loved me, because she cared enough to tell me the truth even when it was uncomfortable. That is what real friendship looks like. It is not just celebrating wins. It is speaking truth. It is showing up in the hard moments. It is staying when walking away would be easier.

I passed Pewaukee, and the lake looked calm. I thought about how still water runs deep. The relationships that matter are not always loud. They are steady. They are quiet. They do not need constant validation to be real.

I thought about the people who have come and gone in my life, the ones who were there for a season and then moved on. That is okay. Not everyone is meant to stay forever. Some people are in your life for a reason. Some for a season. Some for a lifetime. The key is knowing the difference.

I passed Mile Marker 258.2 and made a mental note to reach out to the people who have stayed. To tell them I see them. To thank them for showing up, even when I was not easy to love. Those relationships are rare, and they deserve to be honored.

So here is my encouragement to you: pay attention to who stays. Not who shows up when it is easy, but who shows up when it is hard. Those are your people. They are worth fighting for.

***The people who stay when it's hard are the ones worth keeping.***

# DAY 71

## Mile Marker 287.6: The Weight of Expectations

*"You're not responsible for other people's expectations. Stay true to your calling."*

FREEDOM FROM PERFORMANCE

On the drive to a meeting, my mind was racing. I was thinking about what people expected of me. What they wanted me to say. How they wanted me to show up. Somewhere near Johnson Creek, I realized I was carrying expectations that were never mine to carry.

The highway was busy, full of people heading to their own obligations. I thought about how much weight we carry that does not belong to us. Other people's expectations. Other people's opinions. Other people's definitions of success. We wear them like they are ours, as if we are responsible for meeting standards we never agreed to.

Here is the truth: you are not responsible for other people's expectations. You are responsible for what God called you to do.

I passed a field with a scarecrow standing in the middle, arms stretched wide. It was designed to look intimidating, to scare away birds. But it had no real power. It was just a figure, propped up to create an illusion. That is what expectations are. They look intimidating. They feel real. They have no power unless you give it to them.

I thought about all the times I shaped my decisions around what I thought people wanted. How I edited my words. Filtered my content. Adjusted my goals. Not because God told me to, but because I was afraid of disappointing someone. In trying to meet their expectations, I lost sight of my own calling.

I passed the Pine Cone restaurant and thought about authenticity. The best version of me is not the one who meets everyone's expectations. It is the one who is true to who God created me to be. Even if that disappoints people.

I thought about Jesus. He constantly defied expectations. People wanted a political leader, and He came as a servant. They wanted Him to overthrow Rome, and He preached love. They wanted Him to fit their mold, and He broke it. If Jesus did not meet people's expectations, why do I think I have to?

I passed Mile Marker 287.6 and made a decision. I would not carry other people's expectations anymore. I would not shape my life around what they think I should be. I would focus on my assignment, my calling, and what God placed in me to do. If that disappoints people, that is okay. Their disappointment is not my responsibility.

So here is my encouragement to you: stop carrying expectations that are not yours. Stop trying to be who everyone else wants you to be. Be who God called you to be. Trust that the right people will see your value, even if it does not meet their expectations.

*You're not responsible for other people's expectations.*
*Stay true to your calling.*

# DAY 72

## Mile Marker 292.6: The Discipline of Waiting

*"Waiting isn't wasted time. It's preparation for what's coming."*

ACTIVE TRUST

I hate waiting. I have always been someone who wants things to happen now. Not tomorrow. Not next week. Now. But this morning, as I sat in traffic that was not moving, I was reminded of something I have been learning: waiting is discipline.

The cars ahead of me were at a standstill. An accident up ahead had everything backed up, and there was nothing I could do but wait. I could not control the traffic. I could not make the road clear. I could not force my way through. All I could do was sit and trust that, eventually, the road would open.

I thought about how much life is like this. We want things to happen on our timeline. We get frustrated when God's timing does not match ours. We try to force doors open that are not ready to be walked through yet. But waiting is not passive. It is active trust. It is choosing to believe that what God promised is still coming, even when you cannot see it yet. It is choosing to stay faithful in the in-between. It is choosing to keep showing up, even when the progress is invisible.

I passed a billboard that read, "Good things take time," and I thought about how true that is. Everything worth having requires waiting. Relationships take time to build. Careers take time to grow. Dreams take time to manifest. Trying to rush the process does not speed it up. It usually just messes it up.

I thought about farmers. They cannot rush the harvest. They must wait for the right season, because planting in the wrong season produces nothing. Timing matters, and waiting is part of the process.

The traffic started moving again, slowly at first, then steadily. I realized the wait was necessary, not as punishment but as preparation. Sometimes God makes us wait because we are not ready for what He is about to give us. Sometimes He makes us wait because what He is preparing is not ready yet. Either way, the wait is purposeful.

I passed Mile Marker 296.2 and exhaled. I do not like waiting, but I am learning to trust it. Waiting is not wasted time. It is preparation time. And when the door finally opens, I will be ready.

***Waiting isn't wasted time. It's preparation for what's coming.***

# DAY 73

## Mile Marker 288.2: The Lesson in the Detour

*"Detours aren't setbacks. They're redirections toward where you're really supposed to be."*

DIVINE REDIRECTION

Road closed. Detour ahead. That is what I saw on my drive to work this morning. The signs were everywhere, and all I could do was groan. I had a schedule. I had a plan. This was not part of it. But I did not have a choice. I followed the signs, taking roads I had never been on and adding time to my drive that I had not accounted for.

Somewhere in the middle of the detour, I realized this is a picture of life. We make plans. We set routes. We think we know exactly how to get from where we are to where we are going. Then life says, "Not that way."

The detour took me through a small town I had never noticed before. Quiet streets. A few local shops. Nothing impressive. Peaceful. I thought about how I would have missed this if the road had not been closed. That is what detours do. They take you places you would not have gone on your own. They show you things you would not have seen. They teach you lessons you would not have learned.

I thought about the detours in my own life. The job I did not get that led me to a better one. The relationship that ended and made room for healing. The plan that fell apart and redirected me toward my purpose. At the time, they felt like setbacks. Obstacles. Things that were keeping me from where I was supposed to be. Looking back, I see them differently. They were not setbacks. They were redirections.

I passed a small church with a sign out front that read, "Trust the journey, even when you do not understand it." I thought about how hard that is. We want to understand every step. We want to see the whole map before we start moving. Faith does not work that way. Faith is trusting the detour even when it does not make sense.

I merged back onto the highway, and the road ahead was clear. The detour was over. I realized I did not lose time. I gained perspective. Sometimes the detour is the destination. Sometimes what you learn on the unexpected path is more valuable than what you would have found on the planned one.

I passed Mile Marker 288.2 and made peace with the detour. I did not understand it, but I trusted it. God does not close roads to punish you. He closes them to redirect you. The detour is always part of the plan.

***Detours aren't setbacks. They're redirections toward where you're really supposed to be.***

# DAY 74

## Mile Marker 290.4: The Gift of Anonymity

*"Faithfulness matters more than fame. Do the work, even when no one's watching."*
HIDDEN IMPACT

This morning, my thoughts were on fame, on influence, and what it really means to be seen and known. In that moment, I realized I do not want to be famous. I want to be faithful.

The highway was quiet, and I thought about how many people chase visibility. They measure worth by a following and believe impact requires an audience. That is not true. Some of the most impactful people I know are people no one has ever heard of. They are teachers shaping students in classrooms no one sees. They are parents raising children with no applause. They are friends who show up in hard moments with no recognition. Their work matters, even if it is invisible.

I passed a field where a farmer was working. No audience. No cameras. Just him and the land, doing the work that feeds people he will never meet. That is faithfulness. That is impact. It does not need to be seen to matter.

I thought about the pressure that comes with visibility. People expect perfection when you are public. Every mistake gets magnified. You lose the freedom to be human. There is a gift in anonymity. It allows you to fail without being judged. It allows you to grow without being watched. It allows you to be faithful without the pressure of performance.

Visibility is not bad, but it is not the goal. The goal is obedience. The goal is faithfulness. The goal is to do what God called you to do, whether anyone sees it or not.

I passed a church and thought about Jesus. He often told people not to share the miracles He performed. He withdrew from crowds. He valued solitude over applause. He was not chasing fame. He was fulfilling His assignment. That is what I want to do.

I passed Mile Marker 290.4 and made peace with being unknown—not because I do not want to make an impact, but because impact does not require visibility. It requires faithfulness.

So here is my encouragement to you: stop chasing the spotlight. Stop measuring your worth by your following. Stop believing you have to be seen to matter. You matter because God created you with purpose, and that purpose does not need an audience to be real.

***Faithfulness matters more than fame.***
***Do the work, even when no one's watching.***

# DAY 75

## Mile Marker 246.8: The Measure of Success

*"Success isn't what you have. It's who you're becoming."*

INTERNAL WORTH

Do you ever wake up and immediately start thinking about success? Like, what it means and how we measure it. I realized I have been using the wrong measuring stick. How do we define success? Who decides? My mind went to all the tangible ways we measure it: money, titles, recognition, followers, accolades. None of those things are bad, but they are not the full picture. You can have all of that and still feel empty.

I passed a billboard advertising a luxury car. The tagline read, "Success looks like this." I thought about how we have been sold a lie. We have been told that success is about what you have, what you drive, where you live, and what title you hold. That is not success. That is accumulation.

Success is peace. It is purpose. It is knowing you are walking in your calling. It is going to bed at night with a clear conscience. It is loving well and being loved well. It is internal, not external.

I thought about people I know who look successful on the outside but are falling apart on the inside. They have the house and the car and the title, but they do not have peace. That is not success. That is performance.

As I approached Oconomowoc, I looked to my left at the lake and noticed it was calm. Still water reflects what is above it. True success reflects what is inside you. If you are at peace, it shows. If you are fulfilled, it shows. If you are walking with purpose, it shows. If you are not, no amount of external success will hide it.

I thought about how I have been measuring my own success—by book sales, by engagement, by opportunities—and I realized those things do not define me. My success is measured by whether I am being obedient, whether I am walking in my calling, and whether I am at peace with who I am and what I am doing. Everything else is noise.

I passed Mile Marker 246.8 and redefined success for myself. It is not about what I have. It is about who I am becoming. It is about whether I am faithful, whether I am growing, and whether I am living with integrity. That is success, and it does not need external validation to be real.

***Success isn't what you have. It's who you're becoming.***

# DAY 76

## Mile Marker 277.4: The Cost of Silence

*"Silence isn't always peace. Sometimes it's just postponed pain."*

SPEAK TRUTH

I was driving in silence this morning when a memory surfaced—a conversation I should have had but didn't. Words I should have spoken but held back. Truth I should have shared but kept quiet. And I realized my silence had a cost.

The highway was empty, giving me too much space to think. I thought about all the times I stayed quiet when I should have spoken up—the moments I let fear keep me from saying what needed to be said. Sometimes it was to keep the peace. Sometimes to avoid conflict. Sometimes, because I didn't think my voice mattered. But silence isn't neutral. It's a choice. And sometimes, it's the wrong one.

I passed a church with a sign that read, "Let your light shine." I thought about how light doesn't apologize for being bright. It doesn't dim itself to make darkness comfortable. It just shines. That's what truth does. It doesn't need permission or approval. It just needs to be spoken.

I thought about relationships I've watched deteriorate because no one was willing to have the hard conversation. Problems that festered because no one addressed them. Pain that could have been avoided if someone had just spoken up. You see, silence protects comfort in the short term, but it destroys trust in the long term.

I passed Mile Marker 277.4 and thought about a specific conversation I'd been avoiding—with someone I care about, regarding something that matters. I realized avoiding it wasn't protecting the relationship. It was slowly eroding it. When you care about someone, you tell them the truth—even when it's uncomfortable, even when it might upset them, even when it risks the relationship. You speak up because silence is a slow poison.

I thought about the people who've loved me enough to tell me hard truths—the ones who risked our friendship to speak into my life, who cared more about my growth than my comfort. Those are the people who shaped me, not the ones who stayed quiet to keep me happy.

I passed a field where the morning fog was lifting. The sun was breaking through, revealing what had been hidden in the dark. That's what truth does. It brings things into the light. And while the exposure might be uncomfortable, it's necessary for healing.

I made a decision. I'm going to have the conversation. Maybe not today, but soon. Because the cost of my silence is too high, and the relationship matters too much to let it die from words left unspoken.

You might be facing a similar moment, staying quiet about something that bothered you and letting it create distance in a relationship you once cherished. I challenge you to stop letting it fester. Take time to speak up and give the relationship a chance to mend so healing can begin, even if the scars remain.

***Silence isn't always peace. Sometimes it's just postponed pain.***

# DAY 77

## Mile Marker 302.8: The Rhythm of Rest

*"Rest isn't laziness. It's what makes work sustainable."*

NECESSARY PAUSE

Exhausted. That was me this morning. The kind of tired that sleep does not fix. The kind that comes from months of pushing without pausing. As I drove, my mind went to rhythm, to how everything in creation has a pattern of work and rest.

The sun rises and sets. The seasons change. The fields are planted and then left to rest. Everything has a rhythm. Except me.

I've been going nonstop. Building. Creating. Producing. Convinced that rest is something I'll do later. When I have time. When I've accomplished enough. But "later" never comes.

I passed a farm where the fields were empty. Not because they were abandoned. But because they were resting. Recovering from the last harvest. Preparing for the next planting. And I realized: rest isn't laziness. It's wisdom.

The field doesn't feel guilty for resting. It doesn't apologize for not producing. It understands that rest is part of the cycle. That you can't harvest year-round without depleting the soil. The same is true for us.

I thought about how we glorify busyness. How we wear exhaustion like a badge of honor. How we measure our worth by our productivity. But God didn't design us to run nonstop. He built rest into creation. He modeled it Himself on the seventh day. If God rested, who am I to think I don't need to?

I passed the hospital in Oconomowoc, and I thought about burnout. How it doesn't happen all at once. How it's the result of ignoring your body's signals over and over until it forces you to stop. And I realized: I was heading there if I didn't change something.

I thought about the goals I'd set. The things I wanted to accomplish. And I realized: none of them matter if I burn out trying to achieve them. Because success without health is just delayed failure.

I passed Mile Marker 302.8, and I made a commitment. I was going to build rest into my rhythm. Not as a reward for productivity. But as a necessary part of it. I was going to stop feeling guilty for taking breaks. Stop apologizing for needing recovery. Stop pushing through exhaustion like it's a virtue.

Because rest isn't the opposite of work. It's what makes work sustainable.

So, here's my encouragement to you: if you're running on empty, stop. Not forever. Just long enough to refuel. Build rest into your rhythm. Protect it like you protect your work. Honor it like you honor your commitments. Because you can't pour from an empty cup. And the rest is what keeps you full.

**Rest isn't laziness. It's what makes work sustainable.**

# DAY 78

## Mile Marker 249.6: The People You Outgrow

*"Not every relationship is meant to last forever. Some are just for a season."*

HEALTHY RELEASE

My mind was on a friendship that had ended. Not dramatically. Not with conflict. It just faded. We did not have a falling out. We just stopped having things in common. Our conversations became surface-level. Our connection felt forced.

As I drove, I realized I had outgrown the friendship. Not because they were a bad person. Not because they did something wrong. We were growing in different directions.

The highway curved ahead, and I thought about how we are taught to hold on to relationships at all costs. How we feel guilty when friendships end. How we blame ourselves for not trying hard enough. But sometimes, the most loving thing you can do is let someone go.

I passed a tree that had been struck by lightning. Half of it was dead, the branches bare and broken, but the other half was still alive, green leaves reaching toward the sun. I thought about pruning and how sometimes you have to cut away what is dead so the rest can thrive. That is what outgrowing relationships is. It is not rejection. It is redirection.

I thought about the people who were in my life for a season, the ones who walked with me through a specific chapter but were not meant for the next one. That is okay. Not every relationship is meant to last forever. Some people are in your life to teach you something. Some to help you through something. Some to celebrate a season with you. When that season ends, trying to force the relationship to continue only creates resentment.

I passed Pewaukee and thought about how the lake changes with the seasons. In summer, it is full of life. In winter, it freezes over. It is still the same lake. Relationships are like that. They change. Sometimes they need to freeze to protect what is underneath.

I thought about the guilt I had been carrying. The feeling that I should have done more to save the friendship. The belief that letting it go meant I failed. I had not failed. I had recognized that we were in different seasons. Honoring that truth was more loving than forcing a connection that no longer fit.

I passed Mile Marker 249.6 and released the guilt. I thanked God for the friendship, for what it taught me, and for the season we shared. Then I let it go.

Outgrowing people is not cruel. It is natural. Making peace with that allows both of you to move forward

***Not every relationship is meant to last forever. Some are just for a season.***

# DAY 79

## Mile Marker 285.8: The Mirror You Avoid

*"The mirror isn't your enemy. It shows you what needs to change so you can grow."*

HONEST REFLECTION

I was getting ready this morning, standing in front of the mirror. But I wasn't really looking at myself. I was looking past myself, avoiding eye contact with my own reflection.

As I drove, I thought about why. What was I avoiding? The highway was quiet, and the question sat heavy in my spirit: What am I not willing to see?

I thought about how we avoid mirrors. Not the physical ones, but the metaphorical ones. The people who reflect back what we do not want to acknowledge. The situations that expose what we are trying to hide. The truths we would rather not face. We avoid them because mirrors force us to see ourselves as we are, not as we want to be.

I passed a lake on my right, and the water was so still it looked like glass, a perfect reflection of the sky above. I thought about how reflection requires stillness. If the water were choppy, the image would be distorted. When it is calm, the reflection is clear. That is what happens when we are still enough to face ourselves. The truth becomes clear.

I thought about the feedback I have avoided, the constructive criticism I dismissed, and the patterns people pointed out that I refused to acknowledge. Not because they were wrong, but because accepting their truth meant admitting something about myself I was not ready to face. Avoiding the mirror does not change what is there. It only keeps you from doing something about it.

I passed a church and thought about confession, about how healing begins with honesty, about how you cannot fix what you will not acknowledge. The mirror is not your enemy. It is your ally. It shows you what needs to change so you can grow.

I thought about the areas of my life where I had been avoiding the mirror. The habits I knew needed to change but had not addressed. The relationships that needed boundaries but did not have them. The truths I needed to speak but had not voiced. I realized avoiding the mirror was keeping me stuck.

I passed Mile Marker 285.8 and made a decision. I would stop avoiding the mirror. I would look at myself honestly, not to shame myself, but to grow. Because you cannot become who you are meant to be if you are not willing to see who you are.

***The mirror isn't your enemy. It shows you what needs to change so you can grow.***

# DAY 80

## Mile Marker 262.4: The Weight of Unforgiveness

*"Forgiveness isn't about them. It's about freeing yourself from the weight of what they did."*

RELEASE THE BURDEN

Driving past Sullivan, a memory surfaced. Something someone had done to me years ago. Something I thought I had let go of. But the sting was still there. The anger. The hurt. The bitterness I had been carrying without even realizing it. I thought about how heavy unforgiveness really is.

The highway stretched ahead, and I thought about weight. How we carry things we were never meant to hold—grudges, resentment, pain from wounds that happened years ago but still feel fresh. And we wonder why we are so tired.

I passed a semi-truck hauling what looked like scrap metal—old, rusted pieces of machinery that had outlived their usefulness. I realized we do the same thing. We carry old hurts, old betrayals, old disappointments. Things that should have been discarded long ago. But we hold on to them. We rehearse them. We let them define our present even though they belong to our past. The weight of it is crushing.

I thought about forgiveness. Not the shallow kind where you say the words but do not mean them. The real kind. The kind that releases you from the burden of carrying someone else's debt. Forgiveness is not about them. It is about you. It is not saying what they did was okay. It is saying you are not going to let it control you anymore.

I passed a field where a controlled burn was happening, smoke rising as old growth was cleared to make room for new. Forgiveness is like that. It burns away what is dead so new life can grow. We resist it because forgiving can feel like letting them off the hook, like saying they did not hurt us, like giving them permission to do it again. But that is not what forgiveness is. Forgiveness releases you from the prison of bitterness. It is choosing freedom over revenge. It is trusting that God will handle what you cannot.

I thought about the person who hurt me and how carrying this grudge had not changed anything. It had not made them pay. It had not healed the wound. It had only kept me chained to something that happened years ago. They had moved on. I was the one still carrying it.

I passed Mile Marker 262.4 and made a decision. I was going to forgive. Not because they deserved it, but because I deserved to be free. I whispered a prayer—not for them, for me—asking God to release me from the weight I had been carrying. And I felt it lift. Not completely. Not all at once. But enough to breathe a little easier.

Unforgiveness is a burden you were never meant to carry. Letting it go does not excuse what they did. It frees you from what it has been doing to you.

**Forgiveness isn't about them. It's about freeing yourself from the weight of what they did.**

# DAY 81

## Mile Marker 301: The Power of Proximity

*"You become like who you surround yourself with. Choose your proximity wisely."*
INFLUENCE MATTERS

Recently, I realized something about the people I spend the most time with. I am starting to become like them. Not intentionally or consciously, but gradually, through their habits, mindsets, and perspectives. It is happening whether I notice it or not.

The highway was busy, full of cars heading in different directions, and it made me think about how proximity shapes us, how the people closest to us influence who we become. We become like the people we surround ourselves with.

I passed a construction site where workers were building something together. Each person had a role. Each contributed to the whole. I thought about how powerful collaboration is when everyone is moving in the same direction. But what happens when they're not? What happens when the people around you are moving backward while you're trying to move forward? When they're choosing comfort, while you're choosing growth? When they're settling while you're stretching? You get pulled in their direction.

I thought about the concept of proximity. It's not just physical closeness. It's emotional, mental, and spiritual. It's who you give access to your thoughts, your dreams, your energy. And if those people don't value what you value, they'll drain you without meaning to.

I passed Delafield and thought about a conversation I had recently. They asked why I wasn't hanging out as much—why I'd become distant. The truth was I'd outgrown the relationship. Not because they were bad, but because we were heading in different directions. I had to protect my proximity.

I thought about Jesus—how He had twelve disciples but only three in His inner circle. He loved everyone, but He didn't give everyone the same access. He understood the power of proximity.

I passed Mile Marker 301 and considered the people I was giving access to. Were they pushing me forward or holding me back? Were they speaking life or draining it? Were they helping me grow or keeping me comfortable? I realized I needed to be more intentional about who I let close. Not because I don't care about people, but because proximity shapes you—and I can't afford to be shaped by the wrong influences.

My encouragement to you is to pay attention to who you're close to—emotionally, mentally, and spiritually. You will become like them. And if they're not going where you're going, you'll either pull them up or they'll pull you down. Choose proximity wisely.

*You become like who you surround yourself with.*
*Choose your proximity wisely.*

# DAY 82

## Mile Marker 254.2: The Courage to Start Over

*"Starting over isn't giving up. It's having the courage to build something better."*

NEW BEGINNINGS

This morning, starting over was on my mind, what it means to walk away from something you have invested in and begin again. And I realized something. It takes more courage to start over than it does to keep going in the wrong direction.

The highway was clear, and I thought about all the things we hold on to because we have already invested so much—relationships that are not working, jobs that are draining us, goals that no longer align with who we are becoming. We stay because we have already put in the time, the energy, the effort. And walking away feels like admitting defeat.

But sometimes, starting over is not giving up. It is redirecting.

I passed a sign for a new development: "New Beginnings Start Here." I thought about how every new beginning requires an ending. You cannot start fresh while holding on to what is old.

I thought about the times I have had to start over—the job I left that everyone said I was crazy to walk away from, the project I abandoned after months of work, the relationship I ended even though I had invested years. At the time, it felt like failure, like I was throwing away what I had built. Looking back, I see it differently. I was not throwing it away. I was making space for something better.

Starting over gave me the freedom to build something aligned with who I was becoming, not who I used to be.

I crossed over the bridge with the Crawfish River below me, and it looked different from how it had in the summer. The season had changed, and the landscape reflected it. That is what starting over is—recognizing that the season has changed and having the courage to change with it.

I thought about people who stay stuck in the wrong place because they are afraid of starting over, who endure unhappiness because the alternative feels too risky. But staying in the wrong place does not honor what you have invested. It just wastes more time.

I passed Mile Marker 254.2 and thought about the courage it takes to say, "This is not working, and I am brave enough to try something different." That is not failure. That is wisdom.

So here is my encouragement to you: if you are in a situation that is no longer serving you, do not be afraid to start over. The time you have invested is not wasted. It taught you something. Now take that lesson and build something new.

***Starting over isn't giving up. It's having the courage
to build something better.***

# DAY 83

## Mile Marker 252.2: The Truth About Momentum

*"Momentum isn't built in big moments. It's built in small, consistent actions over time."*

DAILY PROGRESS

Have you ever noticed how hard it is to get started, and how easy it is to keep going once you do? That is momentum. I realized it is built in the mundane.

The highway was smooth, and I was cruising at a steady pace. I was not accelerating. I was not slowing down. I was just maintaining. That is what momentum is. It is not about bursts of energy. It is about consistency.

I thought about how we celebrate the big wins, the launches, the breakthroughs, the moments when everything comes together. But those moments do not happen without the small, unglamorous work that no one sees.

I passed a field where a farmer was working. Same field he had been working for weeks. Same routine. Same slow progress. He was building momentum one day at a time.

I thought about my own work—the books I have written, the content I have created, the goals I have been chasing. None of it happened because of one big effort. It happened because I showed up, day after day, even when I did not feel like it. That is momentum.

I passed a billboard advertising a gym: "Results take time." It is true. You do not get in shape with one workout. You get in shape by showing up consistently over time. You do not build a business with one launch. You build it by serving customers day after day. You do not write a book in one sitting. You write it one page at a time. Momentum is built in the mundane.

I thought about the people who give up because they do not see immediate results, who quit after a few weeks because the progress feels too slow. They are missing the point. Progress is not about speed. It is about direction. As long as you are moving forward, you are building momentum.

I passed Mile Marker 252.2 and thought about the goals I set at the beginning of the year. Some felt impossibly far away, but I have been moving toward them—slowly, steadily. I am closer now than when I started. That is momentum.

So here is my encouragement to you: do not despise small progress. Do not get discouraged because the results are not immediate. Keep showing up. Keep doing the work. Keep moving forward. Because momentum is built in the mundane, and one day you will look back and realize how far you have come.

*Momentum isn't built in big moments. It's built in small, consistent actions over time.*

# DAY 84

## Mile Marker 304.8: Stop Doubting Yourself

*"If you can dream it, you already have what it takes to do it."*
BELIEVE IN YOURSELF

Somewhere between Johnson Creek and Lake Mills, the thought hit me. Not gently. Not like a whisper. It slammed into me like a truck crossing lanes without warning. Stop doubting yourself. Actually, that is not exactly what I heard. What I heard was more direct. More forceful. The kind of language that makes you sit up straight and pay attention.

Stop f*cking doubting yourself.

While the highway was clear before me, my mind was not. It was churning with thoughts about the future. About the next year. The next five years. About all the things I wanted to accomplish. And underneath all of that was something darker—a nagging voice that kept asking, What if you are not good enough?

Despite everything I had accomplished in the last three months, I kept circling back to the same thoughts. Inadequacy. Doubt. Fear that maybe I was in over my head.

I know what people say about profanity. That it is ignorant. That it shows a lack of intellect. That there are better ways to articulate feelings. But in that moment, nothing else would have worked. Sometimes profanity is the only thing strong enough to emphasize the seriousness of a message.

That word cut through all the noise. All the doubt. All the fear. It forced me to face the truth: I was sabotaging myself. Not because I was not capable, but because I was afraid of the unknown.

The truth is, if you can dream it, you have the ability to do it. God does not plant dreams in you that you are not equipped to fulfill. He does not give you a vision without also giving you the capacity to see it through. The dream itself is proof that you have what it takes.

But fear whispers otherwise. Fear says you are not ready. That the timing is not right. That you should wait until you feel more confident. And if you listen to that voice, you will wait forever.

I thought about all the things I had been putting off. The projects I had not started because I was not sure they would succeed. I had not taken the risks because I could not guarantee the outcome. And I realized I was letting fear steal what was already mine.

I was not going to let doubt drive me anymore. I had dreams. Big ones. Scary ones. Ones that felt impossible when I thought about them too long. But I also had everything I needed to accomplish them.

So, stop doubting yourself. Stop letting fear convince you that you are not ready. Stop sabotaging what God already approved. The unknown is scary. But staying stuck in doubt is scarier.

***If you can dream it, you already have what it takes to do it.***

# DAY 85

## Mile Marker 304.2: And the Road Ahead

*"The journey isn't about reaching the destination. It's about who you become along the way."*
LOOKING FORWARD

I pulled into the parking lot at work and turned off the engine. Another drive complete. Another set of miles behind me. But the journey wasn't over. It never is. Tomorrow I'd get back in the car, merge onto the highway, pass the same mile markers, and learn something new. That is what life is: a continuous journey, a series of mile markers that measure not just distance but growth. And I was grateful for every single one.

I grabbed my bag and stepped out of the car. The sun was fully up now, warming the morning. I thought about new beginnings—how every day is a fresh start, a new opportunity to learn, to grow, and to become. Each day I start my journey around Mile Marker 304.2 without understanding what the day will hold. Sometimes, on that journey, the road ahead is full of promise, and sometimes it's not. It's the nature of an unpredictable day.

Traveling the road of life, I have begun to realize that we can never control how our day will go. While we want to have control, life changes so frequently that it doesn't give us permission to say what will or will not happen. And although the lessons of this book are not over, it's a good place to pause and reflect on how far you've come and to understand that there are still miles ahead to encounter and storms to endure.

My mind reflects on all the highways, interstates, and roads that exist in this world. Often they lead from shore to shore, and at the end of a highway there is a body of water. Does the water mean the journey is over? Not necessarily, because it might just mean we need a new method to travel. As you continue forward with this book, rest in these reflections, because as we continue to grow we evolve in how we travel the journey, often captured in wisdom.

Here's my encouragement to you: embrace your journey. All of it. The highs and the lows. The wins and the losses. The moments of clarity and the seasons of confusion. It is all shaping you. It is all preparing you. It is all leading you somewhere.

Trust the process. Honor the mile markers. Keep moving forward. Your journey matters. Your story matters. Every mile you travel is part of a bigger picture you cannot see yet.

So, take a breath. Settle in. Let the journey continue. The road is long, but you are not walking it alone. And every mile marker is proof that you are exactly where you need to be

***The journey isn't about reaching the destination. It's about who you become along the way.***

# DAY 86

## Mile Marker 271.8: Facing the Mirror

*"The only thing stopping you from becoming is you."*

SELF-CONFRONTATION

The highway was empty this morning, which gave me too much time to think. And when I have too much time to think, I end up in a conversation with myself that I am not always ready to have. Today, that conversation was about facing myself.

Not in the literal sense. Not standing in front of a mirror. But in the harder way. In my thoughts. In the battle between what I believe I can do and what I am afraid I cannot.

I passed a field that had been harvested. The land was bare, stripped down to nothing. It looked empty, but I knew it was not. Underneath the surface, the soil was resting, preparing, getting ready for the next season. And I thought about how sometimes we have to strip ourselves down to grow.

The most difficult thing I have had to do in my own life is face myself. Face the thoughts that tell me I am not ready. That I do not have what it takes. That the dream in my head is too big for the person I am right now. Those thoughts do not come from other people. They come from me.

I sabotage myself with my own mind. I will have a vision, a goal, something bold and brave, and instantly, I flip it around. I discredit my potential before I even give myself a chance to try. Why do we do that?

I passed Mile Marker 271.8 and thought about the other side of risk. I have said it before. On the other side of risk is reward. But you have to face the fear first. You have to confront the voice that says you are not enough and challenge it with the truth: God does not call the qualified. He qualifies the called.

The trees along the highway were bare now, their branches reaching toward the sky like they were asking for something. And I realized that is what I needed to do. Reach. Even when I felt empty. Even when I did not feel ready. Because the only thing that stops us from being, doing, or becoming is ourselves. Not other people. Not circumstances. Not lack of opportunity. Us. Our doubts. Our fears. Our refusal to believe that what God placed in us is enough.

I thought about all the times I was willing to do hard things but did not have the willpower to see them through. How I started strong and then let my own thoughts talk me out of finishing. Willing does not always mean able. And able does not always mean I have the mental capacity to push through. That is where the real fight is. Not in the doing, but in the deciding.

I passed the exit for Johnson Creek and thought about all the excuses I had made. All the reasons I had given myself to stop. All the ways I convinced myself that the thing I wanted was too hard, too risky, too uncertain. But what if I faced myself instead? What if I challenged those thoughts instead of accepting them? What if I looked at the fear and said, "You do not get to drive?"

I pulled into the parking lot at work and sat there for a moment. The conversation with myself was not over. It probably never will be. But I made a decision. I was not going to let my own thoughts keep me from what God has for me. I was not going to be the one standing in my own way. Because what God has for me is for me. And the only person who can keep me from it is the one I see when I face myself.

***The only thing stopping you from becoming is you.***

# DAY 87

## Mile Marker 282.2: An Act of Service

*"Sometimes humanity is the best gesture to change the outcome of a person's day."*

CENTERING OURSELVES

Some mornings on the highway between Milwaukee and Madison, I would find myself reflecting on life, who we are as individuals, and what we bring to humanity. During the spring and summer, the drive can feel peaceful. The sun is beaming down, the sky is open, and for a moment it feels like the weight of life loosens its grip. Yet even on those beautiful days, there are moments that shift my attention. I will be heading to a destination I want to reach and see someone on the side of the road. A flat tire. Hazard lights flashing. A person standing outside their car trying to figure out what to do next. On this highway, there are thousands of cars moving in one direction or another, each person on their way to something that matters to them.

As I travel past multiple mile markers between Milwaukee and Madison, there is a part of me that always notices the people who are pulled over. I wonder about what is happening in their day and whether they are scared, frustrated, or simply inconvenienced. One morning on my way to work, I saw a man on the side of the highway with his hazard lights on. His car was tilted slightly, and it was clear he had a flat tire. I saw him from a distance and started to think. How would he respond if I pulled over and offered to help? That simple question took me back to a moment years earlier when I was the one with a problem and someone decided to care.

I was driving on the highway in my truck and had no idea that the hub cap was loose. To me, everything felt normal, but it was wobbling and rattling, getting ready to fly off. A man pulled up next to me on the passenger side and started trying to get my attention. We were both in the flow of traffic, but he kept signaling and pointing toward the front of my vehicle. Eventually I understood that he wanted me to pull over, so I did, and to my surprise, he pulled over behind me. He could have kept driving and stayed focused on his own day, but he chose to stop. He walked up and told me that my hub cap was shaking and looked like it was about to come off. I got out, checked it, and popped it back in place so it was secure again. He stood there for a moment just to make sure I was okay. I thanked him and let him know I appreciated what he did. That quiet act of service reminded me that compassion still shows up on the side of the road and that kindness can be simple. Paying attention. Taking a small risk. Making sure someone else gets home safely.

So now, when I am driving and I see someone pulled over, I think about that man. I think about the gift he gave me by caring enough to stop. It makes me ask myself what it means to pay that kind of care forward. If someone could do that for me, how can I be available to do something for someone else? The challenge is that many of us rarely slow down long enough to give that kind of attention. We are rushing to the next meeting, the next appointment, the next assignment. We will apologize for being late because of traffic, but how many times have we been late because we chose to help someone who looked like they were in distress? That choice says something about who we are and what we value.

You may not be traveling the same stretch of highway as I am, but you have your own road. Your opportunity to serve may not happen on the side of the interstate. It might be in a grocery store when you quietly pay for someone's items when you see them struggling. It might be on an elevator when you hold the door so someone else can make it in. It might be as simple as holding a door open, offering a genuine smile, or checking in on a coworker who looks overwhelmed. Acts of service do not always require money. Sometimes they require time, awareness, and willingness. They invite us to look beyond our schedule and see the person right in front of us. Kindness still has the power to interrupt someone's bad day and remind them that they are seen.

As you travel through your own mile markers, like Mile Marker 282.2 on my route, I want to encourage you to look for one person you can serve in a practical way. Let your life reflect the compassion you have received. Someone helped you before. Someone saw you and cared. Now you have the chance to be that person for someone else.

**Our prayer should always be thank you, God, for those who cared when they did not have to.**

# DAY 88

## Mile Marker 283.6: Elevate Your Brand

*Believe in yourself. Define your space. Control your story.*
PERSONAL EMPOWERMENT

Scrolling through social media the other day, I observed how people show up on their platforms. Some teaching, some performing, some inspiring. And the question hit me: How do you elevate your brand?

The more I thought about it, the answer became simple, but not easy: you believe in yourself.

That's it. None of us can confidently step into rooms, speak on stages, or show up online if we don't first believe in who we are and what we bring to the table. Belief is the root of elevation. It's how you shape your presence, define your lane, and make a lasting impact.

It reminded me of a podcast interview I did not long ago. Some colleagues in higher ed asked, "How are you able to share so much of yourself on LinkedIn and social media?" My answer was simple: strategy and self-belief. On Saturdays, I usually do a brain dump. I take time to pour out my thoughts, ideas, and lessons learned—kind of like this moment right now. From there, I decide what I want to share and how I want to share it. But at the core of that process is belief in my voice, my story, and my authenticity.

Because that's the thing about building your personal brand: you control your narrative. You decide what the world sees. Some people prefer to show only the highlight reel—perfect lighting, perfect captions, perfect life. Others, like me, sometimes show the messy middle too. The moments of doubt, the lessons learned, and what it really takes to grow.

Either way, it's your story. And once you put yourself out there, people will have opinions. Some will cheer. Others will critique. Your job? Keep believing in yourself anyway. Decide which feedback deserves your attention and which deserves your silence.

I passed Mile Marker 283.6 and thought about all the times I almost stayed quiet. All the posts I almost didn't share. All the truths I almost kept to myself because I was worried about what people would think. But then I remembered: my story isn't for everyone. It's for the people who need to hear it. And if I don't believe in it enough to share it, how can I expect anyone else to receive it?

So, here's my encouragement to you: stop waiting for permission to show up. Stop editing yourself down to make others comfortable. Stop hiding your light because someone else might be intimidated by it. Believe in yourself. Define your space. Control your story. That's how you elevate—not just your brand, but your being.

That's my reflection for the day. What about you? What's one belief you need to return to so you can show up more authentically in the world?

***Elevate your brand by believing in yourself first.***

# DAY 89

## Mile Marker 265.4: The Blessing of Delays

*"The Lord will watch over your coming and going both now and forevermore."*
PSALM 121:8 (NIV)

I rushed to Madison that morning and missed my flight. I waited four hours because of my own miscalculation, and even though I accepted the outcome, I wasn't okay with it. I had planned my day and wanted it to cooperate. The drive to the airport was smooth. Construction had settled. The highway was clear. I reached the gate without trouble and finally boarded.

Then the pilot came on the intercom. "It's going to be a loud flight. The landing gear is currently stuck, but it will retract once we're in the air." People chuckled. It was a short hop to Minneapolis, so no one seemed worried. A few minutes later, his voice returned. "We have to make an emergency landing in Rochester. The landing gear is still stuck. We've burned more fuel than expected and do not have enough to reach Minneapolis."

I looked out the window as we lined up to land. The runway lights stretched ahead like a path of tiny stars. Red strobes flashed in the distance. The closer we got, the more I could see it all in detail. Fire trucks idled with hoses ready. Ambulances waited with doors open. Police cars formed a steady line, their lights washing the tarmac in red and blue. I could see the shimmer of heat lifting from the engines and the silver of our wing flexing against the air. My hand pressed against the cool window. I could hear the wheels whining, feel the cabin holding its breath, and then the thud of tires meeting concrete. We rolled, slowed, and came to a safe crawl. Heads lifted. Shoulders dropped. We were okay.

Inconvenienced, yes. Late, yes. But alive. I turned to a fellow passenger and said, "I would rather be here inconvenienced than in the air in an emergency." In that moment, it became clear to me that fate had its own timing. I was not supposed to be in California when I planned. I do not know what I was being protected from. I just knew I had been covered.

That morning taught me something simple and strong. You and I plan our days. We pick the time, place, and activity that will bring us joy. We expect the route to behave. But we never really know what the next hour holds. Delays feel unfair. Yet sometimes a delay is not a denial. Sometimes it is deliverance. What looks like a setback can be safety doing its quiet work. Purpose still moves forward. It just takes a different road.

In that moment, I learned to take a breath and slow down. When we understand that when plans shift we should pause and not become upset, it becomes easier to accept. Doing this allows us to name what we can actually control and release what we cannot. If we do this, it will require us to choose safety over speed.

I want to encourage you to pick the option that protects your peace and the people around you, even if it costs a little time. Let the wait become a teacher and ask yourself, "What might this be protecting me from or preparing me for?" Invite gratitude into that space and let it soften the edge of the delay.

Now reflect with me. Where are you frustrated by an interruption that might actually be protection? What is one small step you can take today to adjust your plans without losing your peace? That is your starting point

***A divine delay is still direction that protects us from the unknown.***

# DAY 90

## Mile Marker 272.4: Tomorrow Is Not Promised

*"Come now, you who say, 'Today or tomorrow we will go to such and such a city, spend a year there, buy and sell, and make a profit'; whereas you do not know what will happen tomorrow. For what is your life? It is even a vapor that appears for a little time and then vanishes away."*

JAMES 4:13-14 (NKJV)

Life is an interesting phenomenon. Every day we wake up, step into our routines, and start expecting certain outcomes. We think, "Okay, today's the day I'm going to get this done. Tomorrow I'll wear that outfit. Next week I'll finally accomplish this."

But then life happens. A monkey wrench shows up and flips everything upside down. It's ironic. We try so hard to control the future, yet the future has a way of directing us.

I'll never forget when this became real for me. A co-worker retired after about thirty years in the industry. She worked hard, sacrificed herself, and put in her time. Retirement was supposed to be her season to enjoy life. Within a year, she got sick, and later she passed away. That shook me.

It made me think about how often we invest decades into work, planning, and waiting for "someday," only for life to rewrite the script. We sacrifice so much for a future that may not unfold the way we expect.

That's when it hit me: tomorrow is not promised. We do not own it. The only thing we can truly control is today. Right now. The opportunities that come today. The people we love today. The joy we can choose today.

Life is a gift. When we stop obsessing over tomorrow or replaying yesterday, we finally understand that happiness is not a destination we eventually arrive at. It is something we choose in the moment.

So, here's my challenge for you: don't wait until retirement, next month, or "when things settle down" to live your life. Start now. Create joy today. Embrace today. Tomorrow will take care of itself.

Maybe it's not a Facebook list for you. Maybe it's a relationship that has run its course. A friendship that has become one-sided. A commitment that no longer aligns with where you're going. Whatever it is, if it is taking up space and not adding value, it is time to let it go.

Because the people who are supposed to connect with you cannot get in if there is no room. The only moment you truly have is this one. Don't postpone joy, don't delay love, don't wait for someday.

***Live fully today—because today is the gift you've been given.***

# DAY 91

## Mile Marker 267.8: How Hungry Are You?

*"Blessed are those who hunger and thirst for righteousness, for they will be filled."*
MATTHEW 5:6 (NIV)

What if I told you I was sick in the hospital and still chasing my dreams? You'd probably think I'm crazy, right? But I'm not. That's my reality. Not too long ago, I found myself back in the hospital with chest pains. Some of you know from my book, *Oakland Hills, Milwaukee Rivers*, that I had a heart attack in 2017. It came back. And in that moment, I had a decision to make: sit at home ignoring the pressure on my chest, or head to the hospital and face it. I chose the hospital.

As the doctors ran tests and searched for answers, I lay there still thinking about my goals, my assignments, my dreams. Because even hooked up to machines, I couldn't shake the truth that purpose doesn't pause. That's how hungry I am. That's how determined I am to walk in what's been placed before me.

You don't have to be in a hospital bed to learn this. Here's the point: you've got to be hungry enough for what you want that life's ups and downs don't derail you. I thought about all the times I wanted to quit. All the moments when circumstances tried to convince me to give up. All the obstacles that looked bigger than my dreams.

Hunger is different from desire. Desire says, "I want this." Hunger says, "I need this." And when you're truly hungry for your purpose, nothing can stop you from pursuing it.

Later that week, driving into the office, I passed Mile Marker 267.8 and thought about that hospital moment. The journey doesn't stop when life gets hard. The mile markers keep coming, ready or not. I realized something: the most dangerous thing you can do is let comfort become more important than calling. The moment you choose ease over assignment is the moment you start dying instead of living.

So, let me ask you: how hungry are you? Are you willing to sacrifice comfort for purpose? Or will you let obstacles convince you to give up?

Here's the truth: your dreams are still waiting on you. Your assignment is still calling your name. And the world needs what only you can bring. Don't let a setback become a stop sign. Don't let a detour become a dead end. Don't let discomfort rob you of your destiny. Stay hungry. Stay focused. Your dreams are still waiting on you.

***Stay hungry. Your dreams are still waiting on you.***

# DAY 92

## Mile Marker 304.4: The Lesson in the Struggle

*"Consider it pure joy, my brothers and sisters, whenever you face trials of many kinds, because you know that the testing of your faith produces perseverance. Let perseverance finish its work so that you may be mature and complete, not lacking anything"*

JAMES 1:2-4 (NIV)

Life gives you the experience you need for the evolution of your consciousness. How do you know it is the one you need? Because it is the one you are having.

Think about the tough seasons you have faced. What were they there to do? They moved you forward. They pushed you to break through what was holding you back and step into who you are becoming, even when it hurt.

That is the truth we miss in the middle of a storm. We get so focused on the pain and confusion that we forget to ask the most important question: What is this here to show me?

This morning, while I was in my thoughts, I reflected on a stretch at work that tested me. It felt like I was pouring out with little satisfaction. Maybe you know that place. The tasks are steady, the pressure is real, and the return feels thin. You wonder if the work matters. You wonder if you still belong. Sitting with it, I realized the season had a purpose. It was shaping my patience. It was strengthening my voice. It was clarifying where I add the most value and where I need to release control.

Every struggle carries a lesson. Every challenge invites growth. When you stop resisting what is happening and start asking what it is trying to teach you, the ground under you shifts. You move from being a victim of your circumstances to a student of your own growth.

Here is how I walk it out now. I pause before I react. I name what I am feeling so I do not carry it in silence. I ask, "What are you here to show me so I can move through this with wisdom?" I listen for the answer. Then I act on what

I learned, even if the step is small. Most times the door forward is not dramatic. It is one faithful decision that leads to another.

The struggle is not here to break you. It is here to build you. Take the blocks life gives you and build something solid while you are still in it. Trust that today's pressure is preparing you for tomorrow's purpose.

As you embrace seasons like this in your life, hold on to this simple prayer to navigate it: *Dear God, in Your infinite wisdom, give me the anointing to navigate this period in my life. If You equip me, I will be able to proceed with the wisdom that only You can grant, stirring the knowledge I know and the knowledge I do not. Amen.*

Every challenge you face is shaping the person you're becoming. Stop fighting the lesson and start learning from it.

**Your breakthrough is on the other side of your willingness to grow.**

# DAY 93

## Mile Marker 296.8: The Mirror We Avoid

*"Search me, God, and know my heart; test me and know my anxious thoughts. See if there is any offensive way in me, and lead me in the way everlasting."*

PSALM 139:23-24 (NIV)

A few years ago, I was in a relationship with someone who was magnetic. Full of life, attractive, driven, and kind. But behind all that brilliance was grief. Deep grief. He was healing... or at least trying to. Processing loss. Carrying weight. Living, but not fully free.

And in one of our deeper conversations, I told him something I now regret: "You haven't fully healed from that." I said it out loud, thinking I was being insightful. In truth, I was immature, maybe even a little arrogant. I had convinced myself that healing should be measured in weeks, months... that there's a timeline. But healing? Healing doesn't follow clocks. It doesn't punch in at 9 and clock out by summer. That was my first mistake—believing someone else should be further along just because I thought they should be.

What I didn't realize then was this: the mirror I was trying to hold up for him... should've been turned around on me. Because I hadn't healed either.

Fast forward—I reconnected with someone new. Someone kind. Considerate. And as we started getting to know each other again, I noticed something strange. There was a wall. Not one they built. One I built. It wasn't physical, but it was real. It blocked me from feeling, from embracing what was in front of me. From trusting, from being vulnerable. And I had to sit with the hard truth: I was still carrying baggage from past relationships. Baggage I had zipped up and stored away, hoping time would heal what I never unpacked.

And here's the ironic part: this new person responded to my unhealed truth the same way I once responded to someone else's. With distance. With "I can't do this," with an exit. It wasn't karma. It was clarity. It was the universe handing me a mirror.

We often say, "I want someone who can be there with me through my healing," but what happens when we are the ones needing that kind of grace? So today, I just want to say this: healing is not weakness. It's work. And sometimes the strongest thing you can do is admit, "I'm not okay. But I'm working on it."

Behind every powerful adult is still that little child inside, waiting to be seen. Waiting to feel whole. And no matter how successful, resilient, or remarkable we look on the outside, the inside still needs nurturing.

I'm on that journey. I'm unpacking the boxes I thought I'd sealed shut forever—the ones labeled "don't open," "too heavy," or "not now." And if you're on that same path—whether you're just beginning or somewhere in the messy middle—I want to walk this road with you. Let's stop hiding what hurts. Let's sit with it. Let's name it. And then, let's heal. The work of healing is sacred, messy, and necessary. You don't have to be fixed to be worthy of love. But you do have to be willing to face what's broken.

**Let's make room for wholeness, one truth at a time.**

# DAY 94

## Mile Marker 289.6: The Open Door

*"See, I have placed before you an open door that no one can shut."*
REVELATION 3:8 (NIV)

Let me share with you a moment of inspiration, motivation, and revelation. On my drive to work one day, my mind reflected on a situation that happened when I worked from home. Usually, during my lunch break, I find myself leaving my apartment to take care of some business, running to the post office, heading to the bank, or grabbing something to eat.

Whenever I leave my apartment, I hear the buzzing of the elevator, which indicates that someone is getting on, or someone has just gotten off. More often than not, I find myself having to wait in order to go to the lower level.

However, this day was different.

When I left my apartment, I heard the familiar buzzing of the elevator. But as I made the turn to get on, the door was wide open, and no one was on it.

It was at that moment that God spoke to me. He indicated that in this season of my life, there are going to be moments when the door is already open. No waiting. No delay. No competition. Just an open invitation to step in.

See, we're so accustomed to waiting, to earning, to proving ourselves worthy of the next opportunity. We expect resistance. We brace ourselves for the struggle. But what happens when God says, "I've already prepared this for you. Just walk in"?

That empty elevator wasn't random. It was a reminder that sometimes the blessing isn't about fighting your way through. It's about recognizing when the path has already been cleared and having the faith to step forward. This happened on April 1, 2025, before the podcasts, book clubs, stages, interviews, and multiple books. It was a glimpse into what God was preparing for me and what I believe He can and will also prepare for you.

So today, I want to encourage you: pay attention to the open doors. The ones that seem too easy, too perfectly timed, too good to be true. Because sometimes God's favor looks like an elevator that's already waiting—buzzing, open, and ready for you to step in.

Not every blessing requires a battle. Sometimes God's favor shows up as an open door with no one blocking your way. When you see it, don't hesitate.

***There are somethings in life prepared just for you only Trust God for it.***

# DAY 95

## Mile Marker 293.4: The Playground of Life

*"A joyful heart is good medicine, but a crushed spirit dries up the bones."*
PROVERBS 17:22 (ESV)

Life is a playground, often filled with cuts, bruises, and scrapes. It has moments of excitement, moments of collaboration, and moments of disappointment. Yet there's always pleasure in being there. Think about it. When you were a kid on an actual playground, you knew the risks. You might fall off the monkey bars. You might skin your knee on the slide. Someone might push past you to get to the swings first. But did that stop you from showing up? Did that keep you from playing?

No. Because the joy of being there outweighed the fear of getting hurt. Life works the same way. Yes, you're going to get bruised. Yes, there will be disappointments. Yes, some days will feel harder than others. But the beauty is in showing up anyway. The pleasure is in participating, in collaborating, in finding joy even when things don't go perfectly.

I think about those same risks now and smile. The point wasn't avoiding pain. The point was learning how to climb again with a wiser grip. Showing up is its own win. Your presence is practice. Practice builds courage. Courage keeps you in the game long enough to grow.

We spend so much time trying to avoid pain that we forget to experience pleasure. We become so cautious, so protective, that we stop playing altogether. But life wasn't meant to be observed from the sidelines. It was meant to be lived—fully, messily, joyfully.

If you need permission to reenter the game, take it here. Start with one small play. One honest conversation. One brave yes. Let delight be data that you are on the right field.

Whenever I drive back and forth to work, passing Mile Markers like 293.4, it allows me to reflect on moments like this. Moments where life challenges us to do and be better.

So, embrace the playground. Accept that scrapes are part of the experience. Find delight in the moments of laughter, connection, and pure aliveness. Because at the end of the day, the greatest tragedy isn't getting hurt—it's never having played at all.

And if you do fall, rise with what you learned in your hands. Wipe the grit from your palms, check your heart, and step back toward the swings. Joy is still possible. Community is still possible. You are still in this. Life will bruise you, challenge you, and surprise you. But it will also delight you if you let it. Show up. Play fully.

***Joy is worth every scrape along the way.***

# DAY 96

## Mile Marker 259.2: The Mystery of Dreams

*"For God speaks again and again, though people do not recognize it. He speaks in dreams, in visions of the night, when deep sleep falls on people as they lie in their beds."*

JOB 33:14-15 (NLT)

Often on my journey, I think about life and the moments of excitement and collaboration it offers. On this particular morning, I decided to go into the office early. Whenever I do this, it usually means I am stressed, and I need time to reset myself and get things off my list. While driving on that highway, I found my mind drifting on the mystery of dreams. It has always been something that has intrigued me over the years, understanding the human psyche and the level of creativity it brings with it.

There have been moments when I woke up out of my sleep and wondered: How did I manage to have superpowers? How did I see the impossible be done? How did I catch a glimpse into the future of what could be possible?

Dreams are fascinating. They do not follow logic. They do not obey the rules of our waking world. In dreams, we can fly. We can solve problems that seem unsolvable. We can visit places we have never been and connect with people we have never met. And sometimes, we wake up with a knowing, a sense that something greater was trying to speak to us.

I believe dreams are a glimpse from God of what our future can behold. They also help confirm what we already have within us to bring that future into reality. Many times, the images we see in our sleep are not random. They are connected to gifts, desires, and callings that God has already placed inside us. The dream simply shines a light on what has been there all along, giving us courage to imagine it more clearly.

What if our dreams are not just random firings of neurons? What if they are windows into possibility? What if they are God's way of showing us what we are capable of when we stop limiting ourselves with what seems realistic or practical? When we treat dreams as holy hints instead of strange stories, they move from entertainment to invitation. They push us to ask, "What is God trying to show me about myself, my future, or the people I am called to serve?"

See, in our waking hours, we are bound by doubt, by fear, by what others tell us is possible. But in our dreams, those boundaries disappear. We become limitless. And maybe that is the point. Maybe dreams are reminders that we were designed for more than what we have settled for. They nudge us to confront the small version of ourselves we carry into meetings, relationships, and decisions, and to consider that God sees someone much bigger.

So, pay attention to your dreams, not just the ones you have while sleeping, but the ones that wake you up with possibility. The visions that stir something deep inside you. Because those are not accidents. They are invitations to step into a version of yourself that has been waiting to emerge. When you wake up from a dream that will not let you go, do not shrug it off. Pray about it. Write it down. Ask God what step you can take, even a small one, to walk toward what He has shown you.

Your dreams—both sleeping and waking—hold clues to who you're meant to become. Don't dismiss them as impossible. Let them stretch your vision of what's possible.

***You were made for more than you've imagined.***

# DAY 97

## Mile Marker 284.6: You Deserve Better

*"Forget the former things; do not dwell on the past. See, I am doing a new thing! Now it springs up; do you not perceive it?"*

ISAIAH 43:18-19 (NIV)

You have the power to rewrite the chapters of your life—don't let the past define you; let your decisions create your future. Who would have known, the road that I travel each day to work is like life – rocky, unpredictable, and rough. Sometimes you find yourself driving through fog, unsure of where you're headed. Other times, you glance in the rearview mirror and see reminders of where you've been — mistakes, detours, and potholes that left their mark. But here's the truth: the same road that once carried your pain can also lead you toward your purpose.

We've all made mistakes, faced setbacks, or experienced disappointments. It's part of being human. But just because the past holds certain chapters doesn't mean those chapters define who we are. The beauty of life is that we have the power to rewrite our story, starting with the next decision we make.

Sometimes we hold on to the past as though it's a weight we can never shake off. We believe that past mistakes or missed opportunities will forever determine our future. But in reality, the past is just that — the past. It's already been written. The real power lies in the choices you make today, and those choices shape the miles still ahead.

Don't let fear of failure or regret hold you back. If you don't like where your story is headed, you have the power to change direction. The key is to make decisions with intention — to choose the path that aligns with who you want to become. Every new chapter is an opportunity for growth, and no matter what happened before, you can always start fresh.

It's never too late to rewrite your story. Whether it's changing careers, building new relationships, or pursuing a long-forgotten dream, the power to create your future is in your hands. Each decision, no matter how small, can change the direction of your life.

So, stop letting the past hold you hostage. Look ahead. The road may have curves, but every turn offers a new beginning. Embrace the power to rewrite your life's narrative — because the future is yours to create.

***The past is a mile behind you; the next decision determines the road ahead.***

# DAY 98

## Mile Marker 247.8: The Beauty of the Journey

*"Your story isn't just about the destination—it's about the journey. Embrace each step, and let it shape the masterpiece you're creating."*

REFLECTION

On this morning, something was resting on me heavy. My day began normal, but then something shifted when I got in my car because I started reflecting on life pretty heavy. Like on my daily drives, I'm heading to a particular destination. Sometimes it's a quick trip, and other times not so much. However, my end goal is always the destination. I pass several mile markers on this journey, and it never fails that at some point I just want to get there and forget to see the other things that are a part of it.

Why? It's sad that in our fast-paced world, we often focus too much on the destination. Whether it's achieving a career goal, reaching personal milestones, or finding success, we tend to measure our progress by the end result. But what if we took a moment to pause and appreciate the journey itself? I felt that question sit with me as the highway opened up. Fields slid by in quiet color. The sky lifted its soft light. A familiar mile marker flashed blue on my right, and I realized I almost missed it again—the small proof that I was moving, even when I did not feel it.

The truth is, the journey is where real growth happens. Each step you take, each lesson you learn, and each challenge you overcome adds depth to your story. These moments, however small, shape the person you're becoming. Success isn't just about reaching the finish line. It is about how you grow, adapt, and evolve along the way. I thought about conversations that changed my tone, detours that taught me patience, and quiet mornings that reminded me to breathe. None of those looked like a finish line, yet each one moved me forward.

As you move forward in this new chapter, take the time to savor each step of the journey. Celebrate the progress you make, no matter how small, and learn from the challenges you face. Embrace the process, knowing that it's not the destination that defines your story, but the way you navigate the journey. If today only offers you one faithful step, take it. Name it. Let it count. Tomorrow will have its own step.

The masterpiece you're creating isn't just about the end result. It is about every moment you experience, every decision you make, and every person you become along the way. Keep writing your story with intention. Notice the mile markers that prove you are still in motion. Wave at the simple graces that show up in ordinary places. Trust that the road is shaping you while you are on it, not only when you arrive.

***Growth happens between the milestones—don't rush the process that's shaping your masterpiece.***

# DAY 99

## Mile Marker 241.4: What Will You Create?

*"The Lord directs the steps of the godly. He delights in every detail of their lives."*
PSALM 37:23 (NLT)

Every morning feels like a new beginning, a blank page waiting to be written. As I get dressed and head out on the road, I am reminded that the possibilities are endless. The sky lifts its soft light, coffee warms my hands, and the first few miles feel like a quiet promise. Each sunrise reminds me that life hands us another opportunity to write a better story than we did the day before. Unlike a script that is already written, this one is ours to shape. Every decision, every action, every word becomes a sentence that defines who we are becoming.

But how often do we stop and think about what we are writing? I ask myself that as the mile markers slip by. Am I choosing words that heal or words that harm? Am I acting from purpose or from hurry? When I pause long enough to choose with care, I remember that each moment carries weight. Each day I drive forward through new moments, conversations, and choices that set the direction of my journey, even when the changes feel small.

The key to a meaningful life story is intentionality. When I live with purpose, my choices line up with my vision. I start to see that my words, my habits, and even my responses in difficult moments are part of something greater. The story becomes less about perfection and more about growth. It becomes less about speed and more about substance. I can breathe a little easier when I remember that steady steps still count.

And when detours come, I remind myself they are part of the masterpiece. There are mornings when traffic slows me to a crawl, or a sudden storm forces me to turn on the wipers and lean in. How I respond to the setback or the stillness reveals a resilience I did not know I had. The pause does not erase the journey. It deepens it.

So today, take a moment to reflect. What story are you writing with your life? Will your words, choices, and steps lead you toward the vision you hold in your heart, or pull you off course? The pen is in your hands. Write boldly. Live intentionally. Notice the mile markers that prove you are still moving. Remember this too: every mile matters.

***The blank page is yours to fill—choose the words of your story wisely, for each one holds the power to shape your future.***

# DAY 100

## Mile Marker 240.0: Make Yourself Proud

*"With every choice you make, you are creating the future you will one day look back on—make it one you'll be proud of."*

CONFIDENCE

Life is like a long drive home after a rough day in the office, a series of turns, stops, and stretches that test both your patience and direction. As we travel through our daily routines, it's easy to get caught up in the next mile and forget to look around at the view along the way. Every small choice, every decision at a fork in the road, is shaping the destination we'll one day arrive at, and the story we'll tell when we look back.

Each decision is like a brushstroke on the canvas of your life. You may not see the full picture in the moment, but over time, those small choices come together to form something meaningful. The beauty of this process is that you have control over how the painting, or the road ahead, unfolds. You can choose to drive with intention or coast without direction.

Imagine looking back on your journey years from now. What do you want to see in the rearview mirror? What kind of person do you want to have become? These questions help you steer your life with purpose. When your choices align with your values and dreams, you're paving a road you'll be proud to have traveled.

As you move into this next stretch of life, remember that every turn counts. Whether it's a small adjustment or a bold change, each one moves you closer to the future you're building. Stay intentional. We've now reached Mile Marker 240.0, the end of my daily commute. The next destination is a mystery, but the beauty is that we get to choose the route that leads toward the person you're meant to become.

Here is what I know from this road. Silence taught me to listen. Detours taught me to trust. Delays taught me to breathe. Pivots taught me that forward can look different than planned and still be right. Letting go made room for what fit. Endurance built strength I could not see until I needed it. Small joys kept me human on heavy days. Protection met me in ways I did not always recognize in the moment. Every mile had a lesson. Every lesson became a marker. Each marker made me.

So, before we close this day's drive, look with me. In the rearview are the places you survived. On the dash is the grace that kept you here. Out the windshield is a road that still opens, even when it bends. You do not have to see the whole map to take the next faithful mile. Choose the lane that honors who you are becoming. Set your pace. Keep your peace. Let purpose be your passenger and gratitude your fuel.

If you ever wonder whether your life is adding up, check the markers. You are further than you think. You are stronger than you were. You are not traveling alone. And the same God who kept you through rain, ice, and night will keep you through what comes next.

When you reach tonight's exit, park the car, step out, and feel the ground hold you. Breathe. Name one mile you are grateful for. Then rest. Tomorrow there will be new light, new road, and new chances to choose well. Your story is still being written in real time by the steps you take with intention.

I'll meet you somewhere up the highway. Different sky. New mile. Same grace. Be encouraged because purpose awaits with each mile you drive.

***Drive your life with purpose, every decision is a mile toward the version of you that you'll be proud to meet.***

**GOD IS WITH YOU**

AT EVERY MILE MARKER.

240.0

# ABOUT THE AUTHOR

Keyimani L. Alford, PhD. is an author, publisher, and Associate Vice President of Student Access & Success at Madison College. For 25 years he has advanced equity, developed leaders, and helped underrepresented voices claim their stories. Through Keywords Unlocked, he equips aspiring authors—especially Black voices—to navigate self-publishing with clarity.

His work includes *Oakland Hills, Milwaukee Rivers: A Memoir of Survival, Identity, and Purpose*, *Unshaken Leadership: A Practical Blueprint for Overcoming Challenges, Learning from Mistakes, and Growing in Confidence*, and *Self-Publishing from Scratch: A Practical Guide for Authors to Publish Successfully with Insights for Black Voices*, along with companion journals and workbooks. Known for authenticity and a dignity-first approach, Dr. Key blends personal storytelling with actionable tools that lead to real-world outcomes—growth, resilience, and confident leadership. He speaks at campuses, conferences, and community events, inviting audiences to reconnect with purpose and take the next step forward. Connect at DrKeySpeaks.com or KeywordsUnlocked.com.

# ACKNOWLEDGMENTS

I am grateful to God for guiding me through every mile marker of this journey. His physical and spiritual covering has been monumental in my growth as a believer. Thank You for protecting me each time the tires of my car hit the road and for keeping me steady when challenges tried to stop me.

To my family, friends, colleagues, and readers who believed in me, prayed for me, and encouraged this work into existence, thank you. You know who you are.

I also want to honor the memory of my friend, Schunn Ferguson, who once drove out to pick me up from the side of the road when my tire came off on the highway. That day became a mile marker of protection and brotherhood that I will never forget. Thank you for being there, and may your legacy continue to live on in our hearts.

# ADDITIONAL PUBLICATIONS

*Oakland Hills, Milwaukee Rivers: A Memoir of Survival, Identity, and Purpose*

A deeper, expanded memoir on survival, identity, faith, and healing.

*The Healing Companion*

A guided journal to process your own healing alongside OHMR and walk more intentionally through your story.

*Self-Publishing from Scratch: A Practical Guide for Authors to Publish Successfully with Insights for Black Voices*

A step-by-step guide through the publishing process for authors.

*OHMR Workbook: A Guide for Faith and Biblical Application*

Scripture-based questions and prompts to connect OHMR to God's Word.

*Unshaken Leadership*

Practical leadership lessons for navigating pressure, politics, and personal growth.

*Unshaken Leadership Workbook*

Companion exercises and reflections to apply Unshaken Leadership in real life.

www.ingramcontent.com/pod-product-compliance
Lightning Source LLC
Chambersburg PA
CBHW020926090426
42736CB00010B/1057